COWBOYS & ALIENS®

PROLOGUE

Writer
Andrew Foley

Art and Colors
Dennis Calero

GRAPHIC NOVEL

Writers
Fred Van Lente & Andrew Foley

Penciller
Luciano Lima and Magic Eye Studios

Inkers
J. Wilson
Silvio Spotti
Luciano Kars
Magic Eye Studios

Colors
Andrew Elder

Letters
Scott O. Brown

Title & Book Design
Zachary Pennington

COWBOYS & ALIENS
created by Scott Mitchell Rosenberg

itbooks
AN IMPRINT OF HARPERCOLLINSPUBLISHERS

PLATINUM STUDIOS COMICS
PLATINUM STUDIOS, INC.
LOS ANGELES, CALIFORNIA

FIRST IT BOOKS EDITION PUBLISHED 2011.

EVERY CONQUEROR BELIEVES HIMSELF MOVED BY A HIGHER POWER. THE IMPERIALIST'S ACTIONS ARE ALWAYS JUSTIFIED, BY NECESSITY, COMPASSION, OR DIVINE PROVIDENCE.

FOR THOSE WHO BELIEVED IN IT, MANIFEST DESTINY WAS A NOBLE ENDEAVOR--A GOD-GIVEN DUTY TO SPREAD THE PRINCIPLES OF THE UNITED STATES THROUGHOUT THE WORLD IN GENERAL...

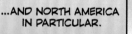

...AND NORTH AMERICA IN PARTICULAR.

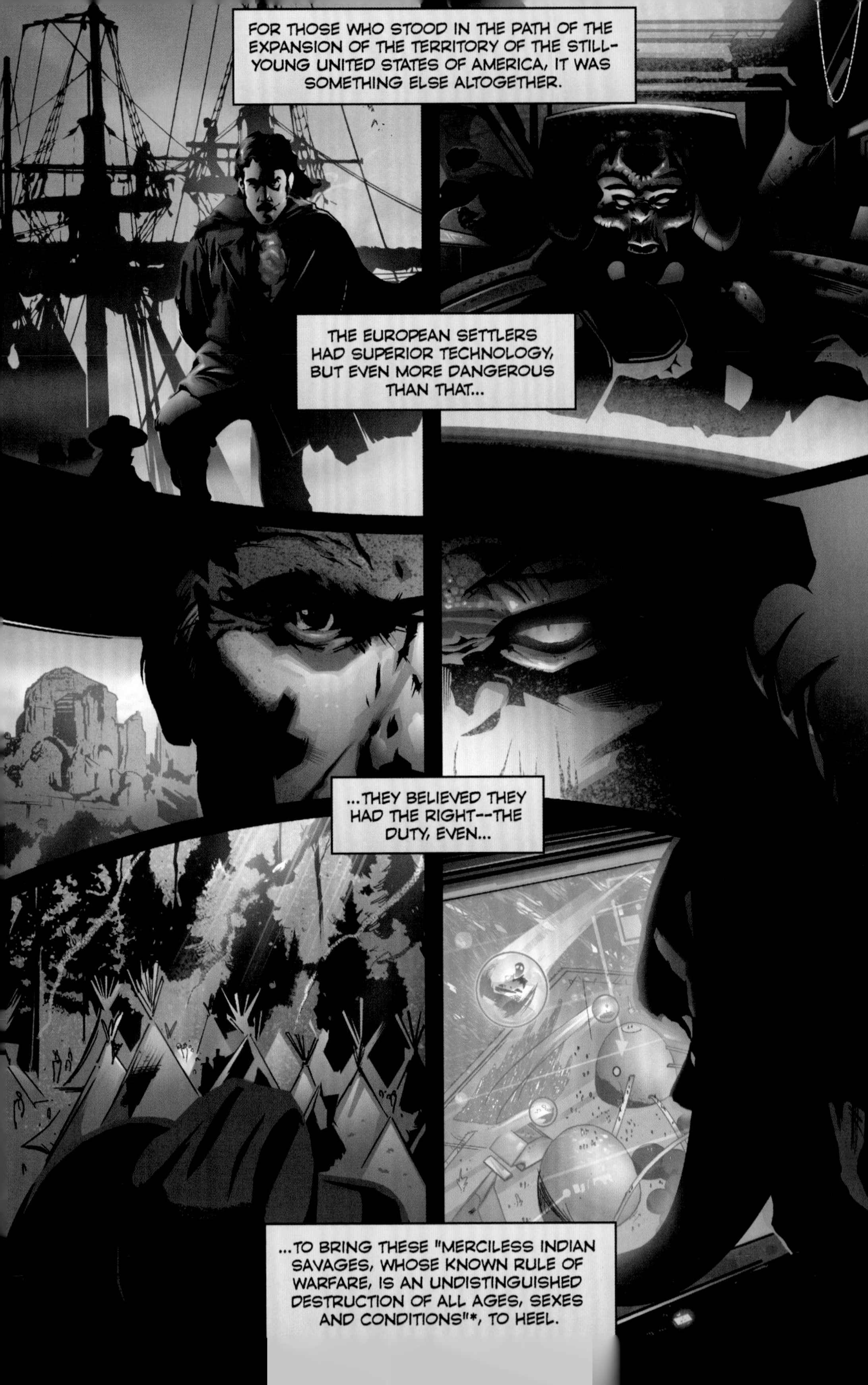
FOR THOSE WHO STOOD IN THE PATH OF THE EXPANSION OF THE TERRITORY OF THE STILL-YOUNG UNITED STATES OF AMERICA, IT WAS SOMETHING ELSE ALTOGETHER.
THE EUROPEAN SETTLERS HAD SUPERIOR TECHNOLOGY, BUT EVEN MORE DANGEROUS THAN THAT...
...THEY BELIEVED THEY HAD THE RIGHT--THE DUTY, EVEN...
...TO BRING THESE "MERCILESS INDIAN SAVAGES, WHOSE KNOWN RULE OF WARFARE, IS AN UNDISTINGUISHED DESTRUCTION OF ALL AGES, SEXES AND CONDITIONS"*, TO HEEL.

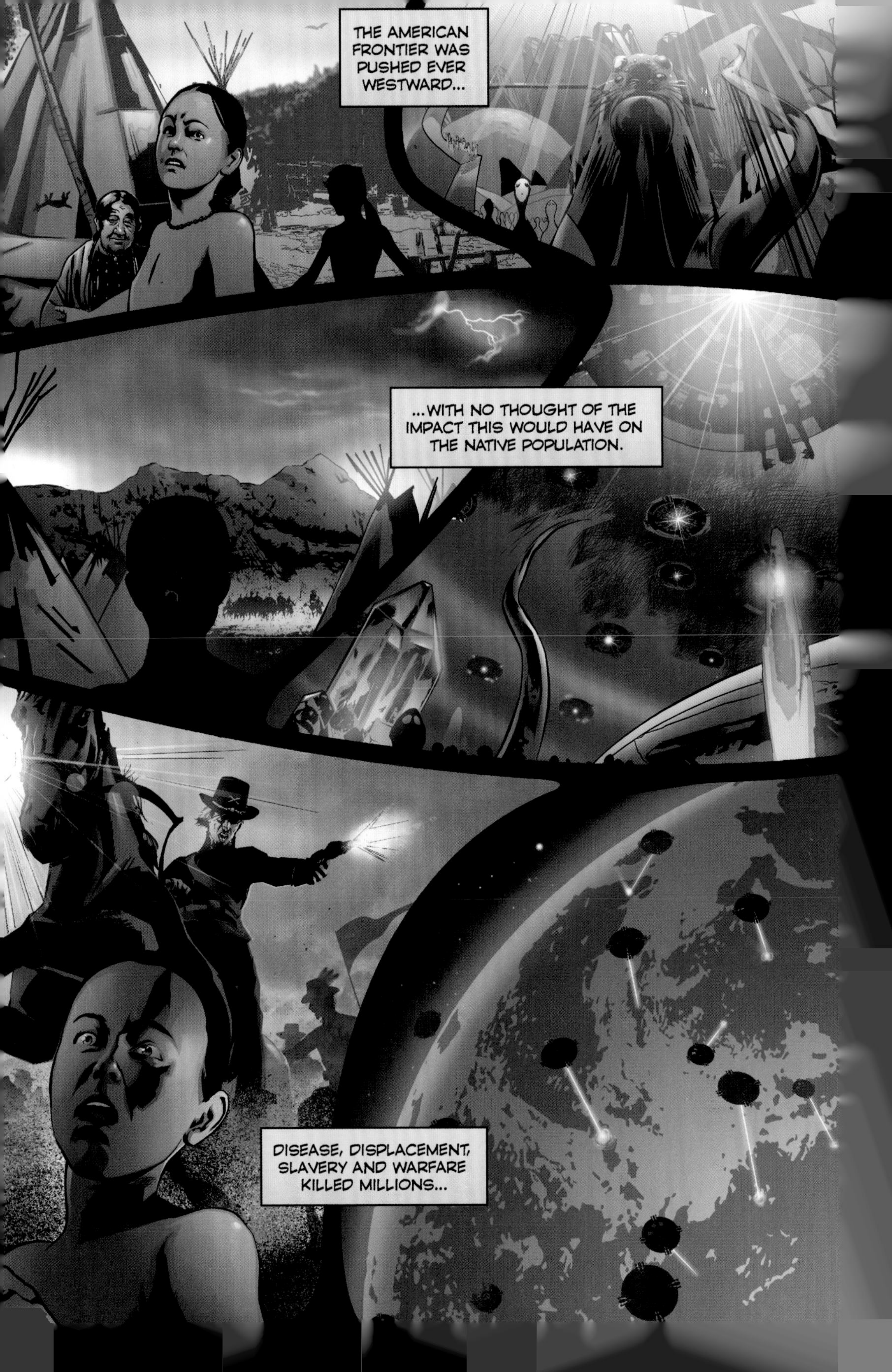
THE AMERICAN FRONTIER WAS PUSHED EVER WESTWARD...
...WITH NO THOUGHT OF THE IMPACT THIS WOULD HAVE ON THE NATIVE POPULATION.
DISEASE, DISPLACEMENT, SLAVERY AND WARFARE KILLED MILLIONS...

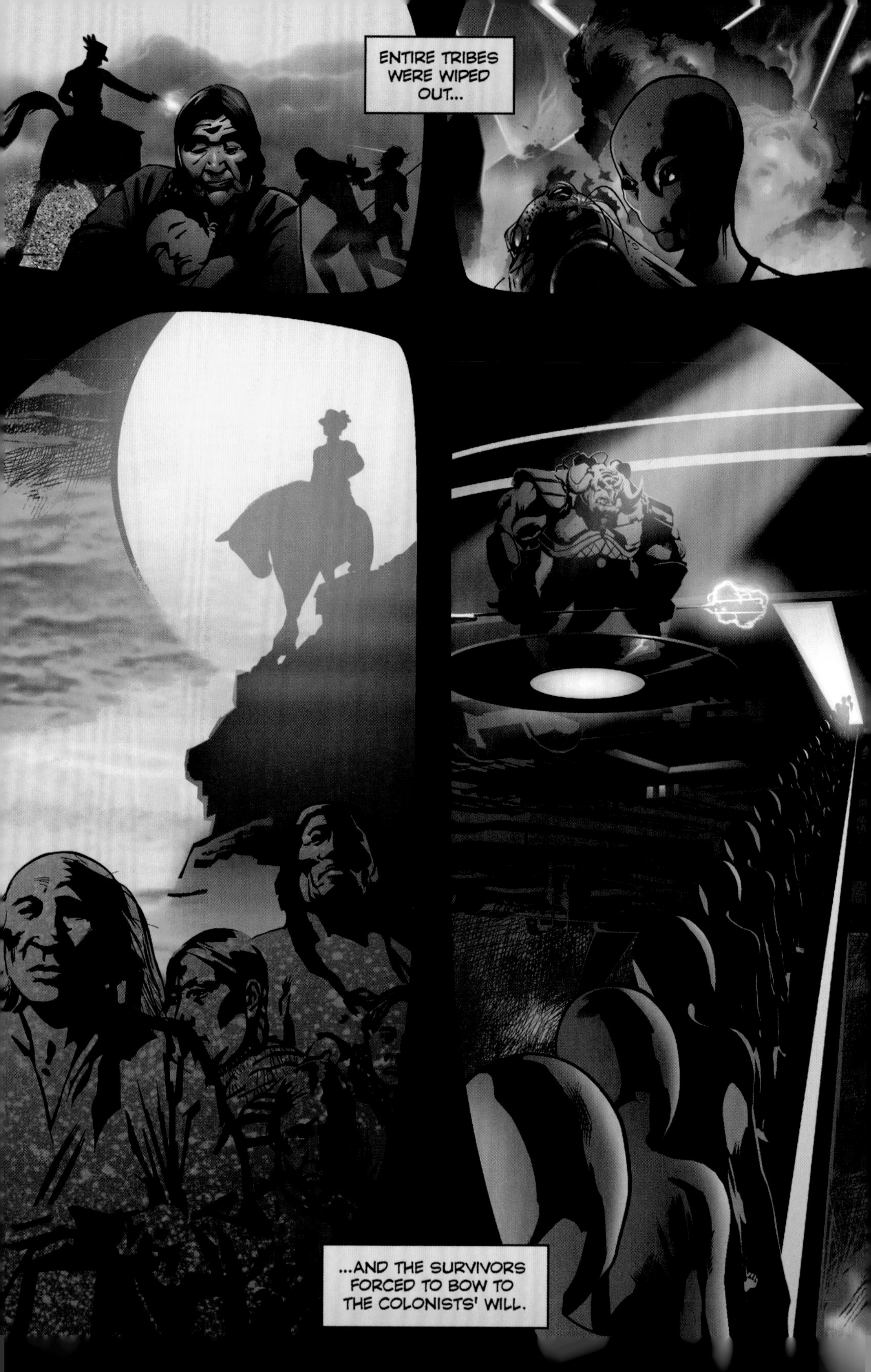
ENTIRE TRIBES WERE WIPED OUT...
...AND THE SURVIVORS FORCED TO BOW TO THE COLONISTS' WILL.

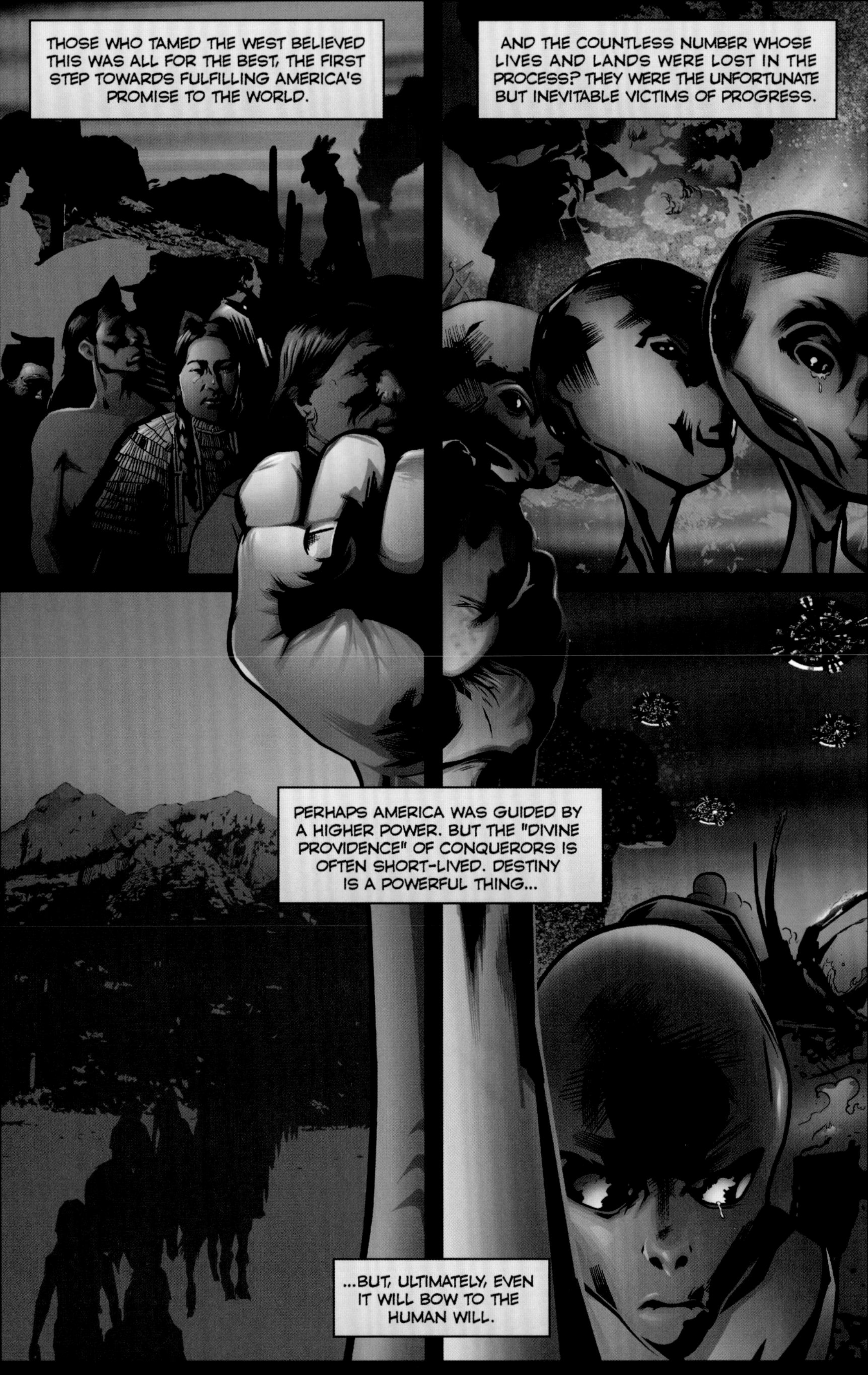
THOSE WHO TAMED THE WEST BELIEVED THIS WAS ALL FOR THE BEST, THE FIRST STEP TOWARDS FULFILLING AMERICA'S PROMISE TO THE WORLD.
AND THE COUNTLESS NUMBER WHOSE LIVES AND LANDS WERE LOST IN THE PROCESS? THEY WERE THE UNFORTUNATE BUT INEVITABLE VICTIMS OF PROGRESS.
PERHAPS AMERICA WAS GUIDED BY A HIGHER POWER. BUT THE "DIVINE PROVIDENCE" OF CONQUERORS IS OFTEN SHORT-LIVED. DESTINY IS A POWERFUL THING...
...BUT, ULTIMATELY, EVEN IT WILL BOW TO THE HUMAN WILL.

The Old West
1873

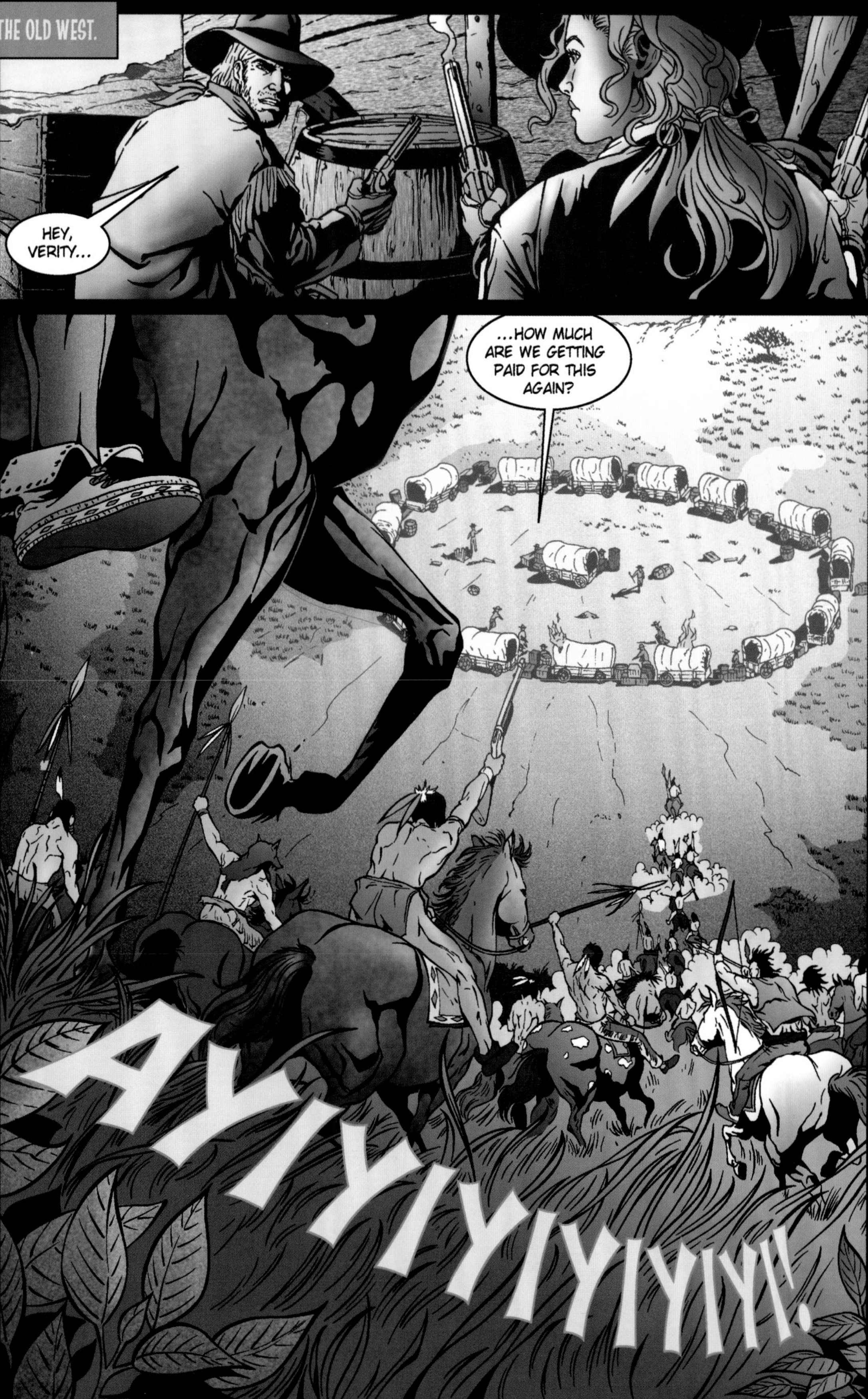
THE OLD WEST.
HEY, VERITY...
...HOW MUCH ARE WE GETTING PAID FOR THIS AGAIN?
AYIYIYIYIYIYI!

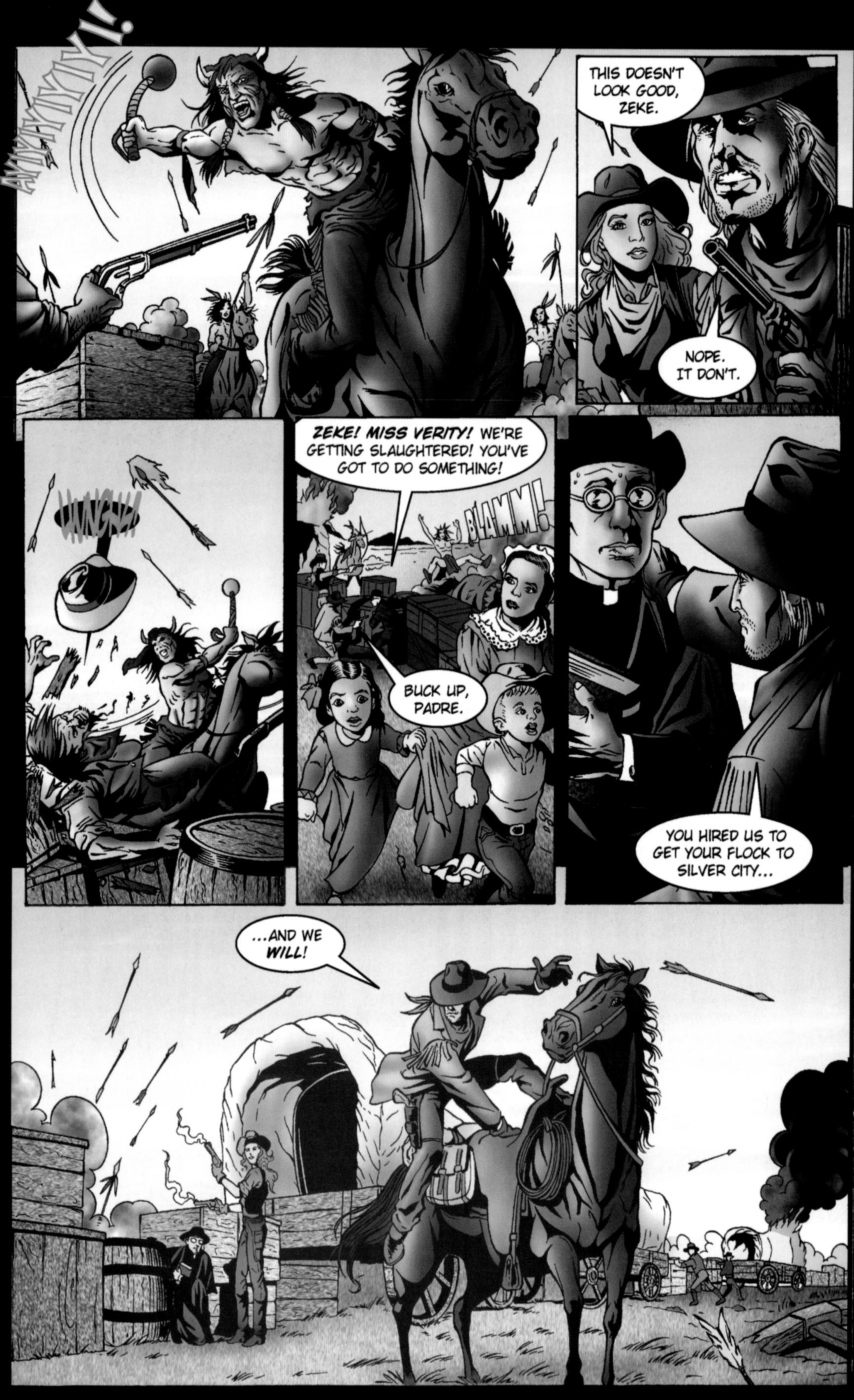
THIS DOESN'T LOOK GOOD, ZEKE.
NOPE. IT DON'T.
ZEKE! MISS VERITY! WE'RE GETTING SLAUGHTERED! YOU'VE GOT TO DO SOMETHING!
BLAMM!
BUCK UP, PADRE.
YOU HIRED US TO GET YOUR FLOCK TO SILVER CITY...
...AND WE WILL!

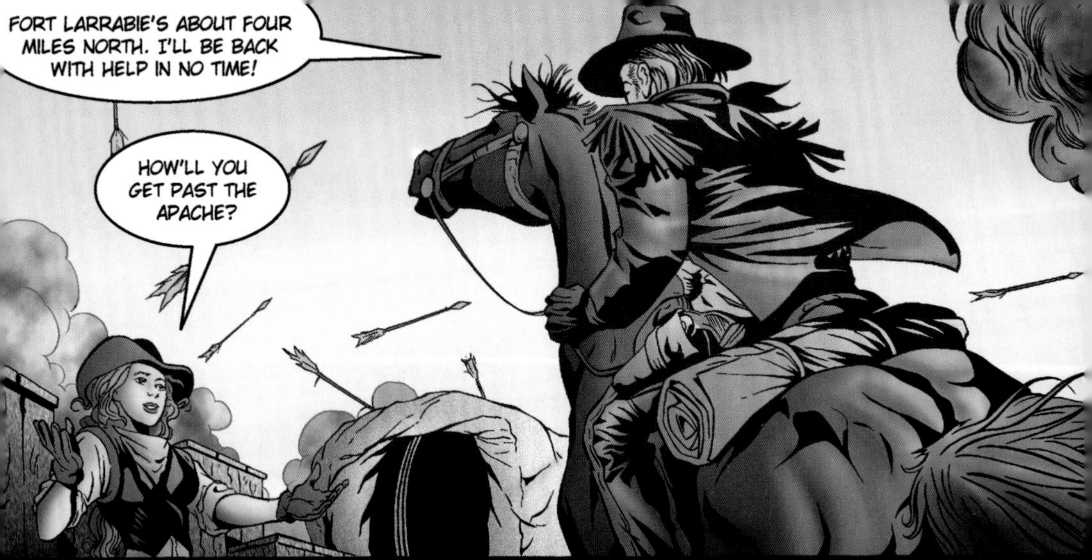
FORT LARRABIE'S ABOUT FOUR MILES NORTH. I'LL BE BACK WITH HELP IN NO TIME!
HOW'LL YOU GET PAST THE APACHE?

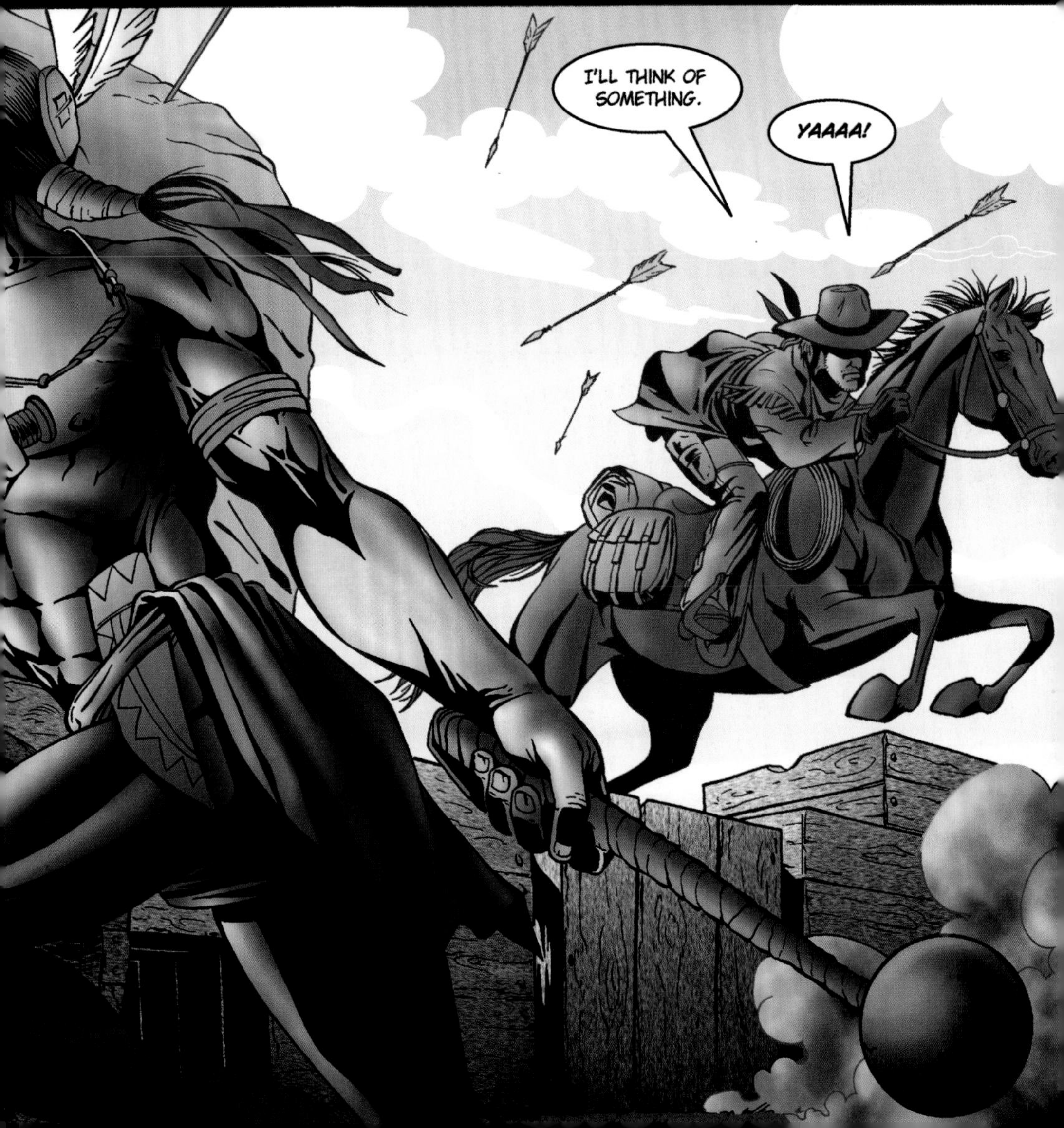
I'LL THINK OF SOMETHING.
YAAAA!

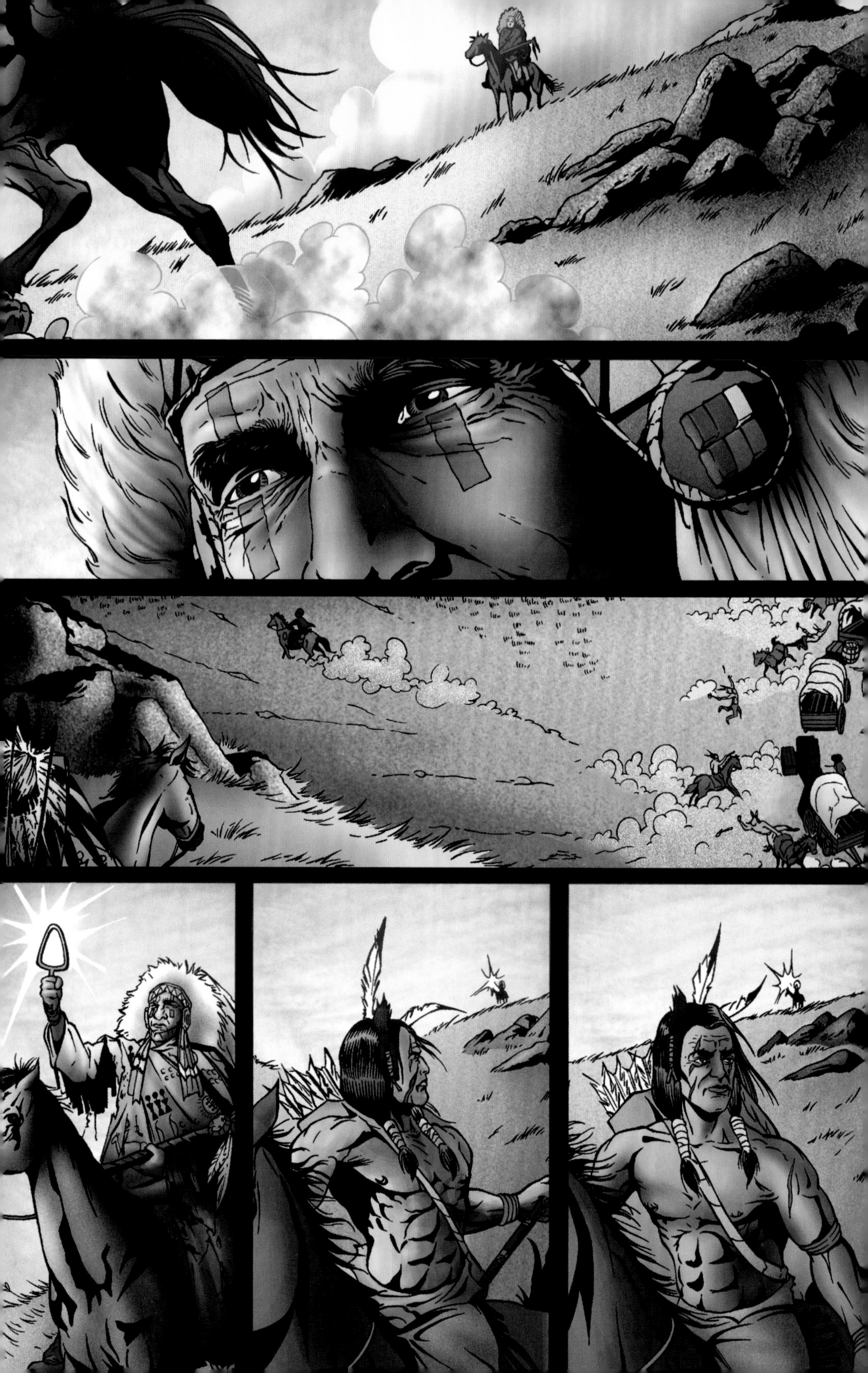

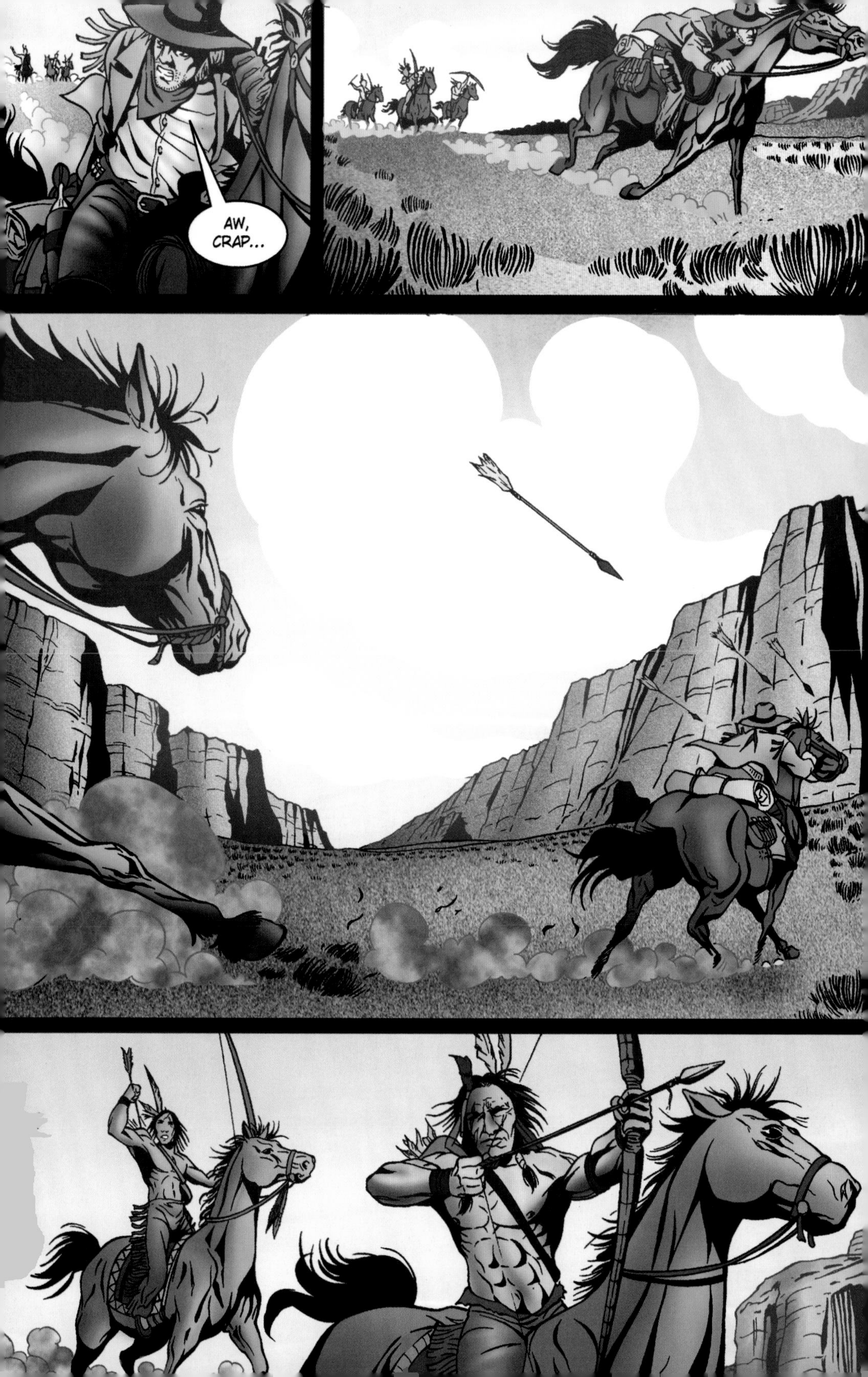
AW, CRAP...

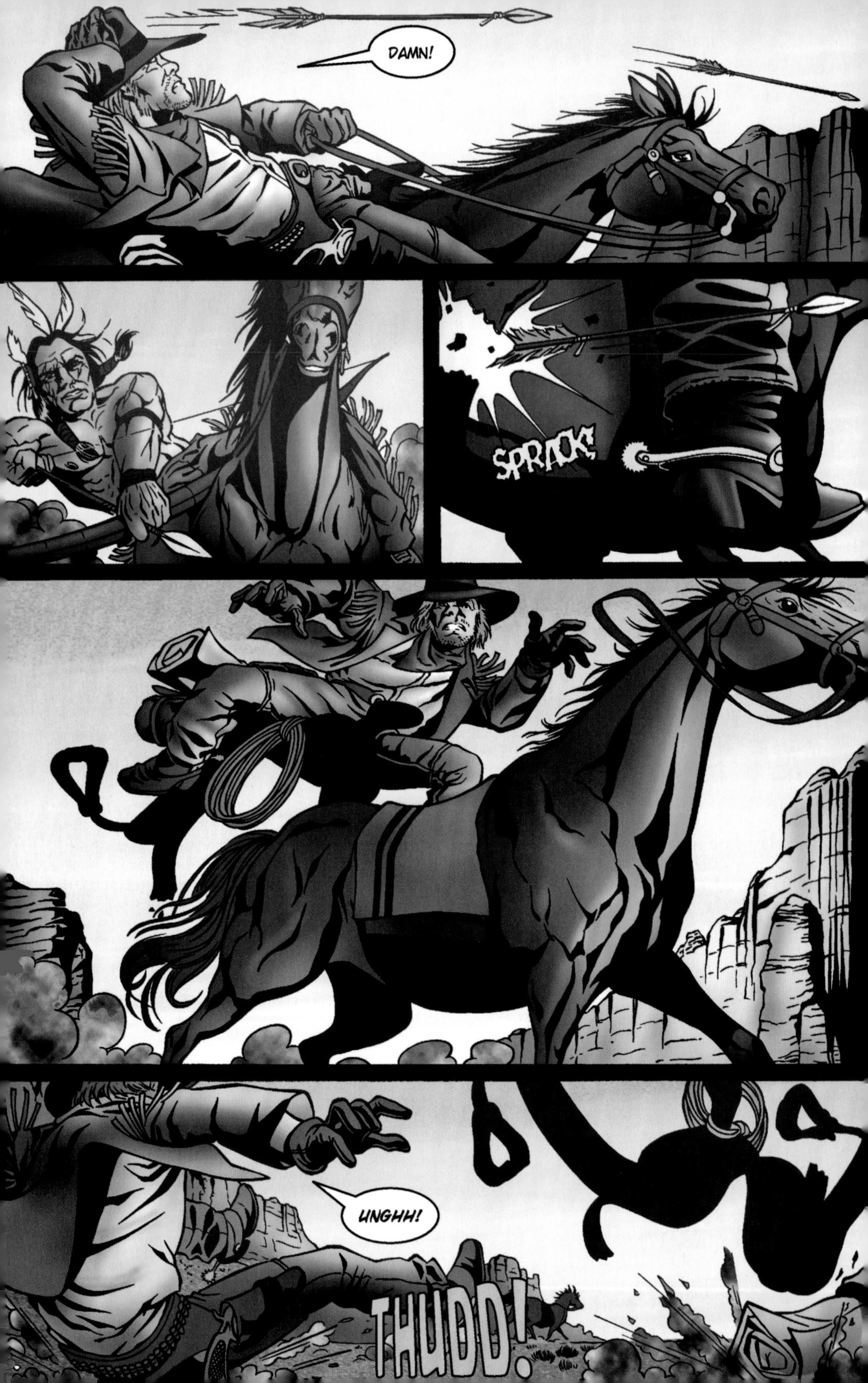
DAMN!
SPRACK!
UNGHH!
THUDD!

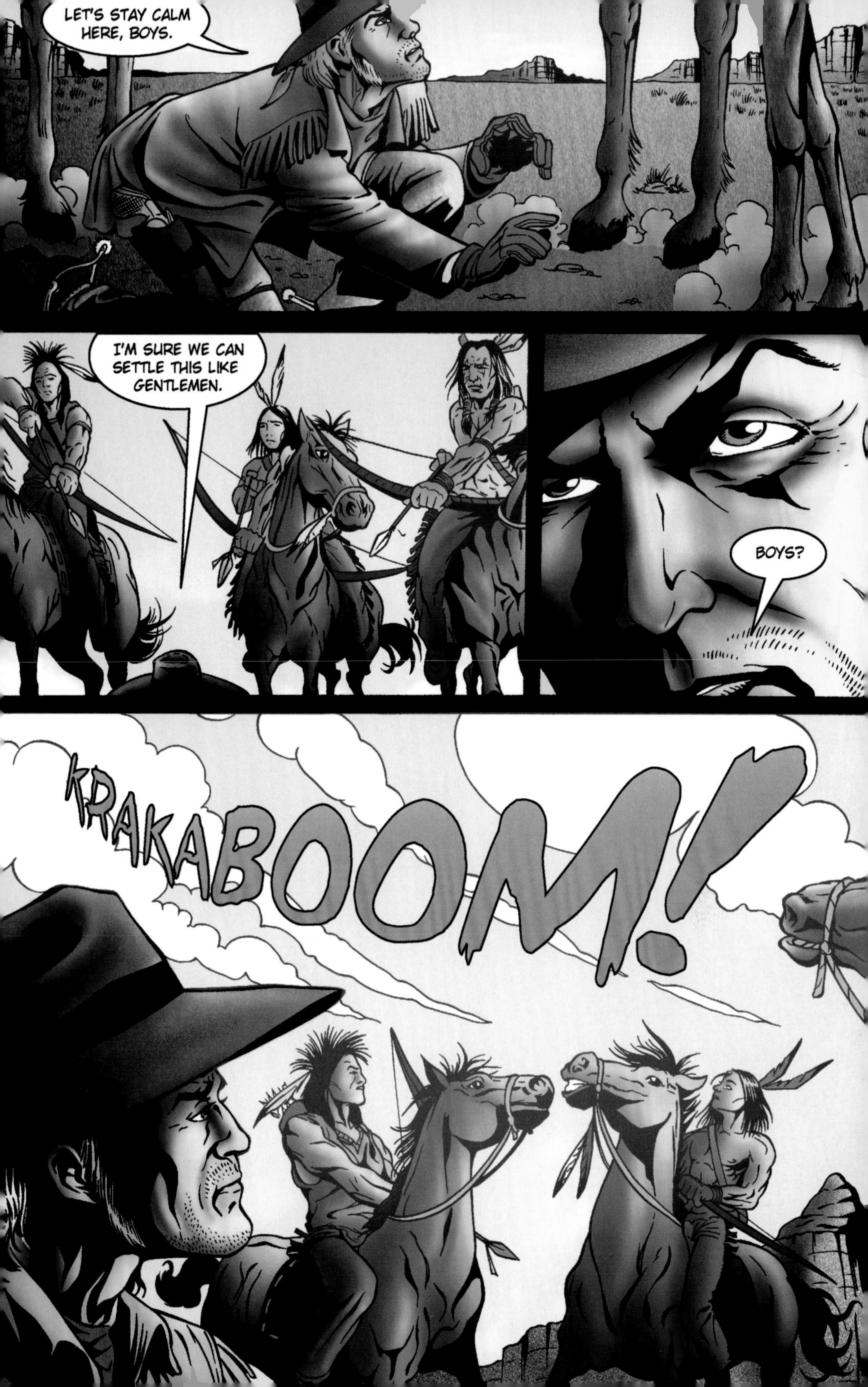
LET'S STAY CALM HERE, BOYS.
I'M SURE WE CAN SETTLE THIS LIKE GENTLEMEN.
BOYS?
KRAKABOOM!

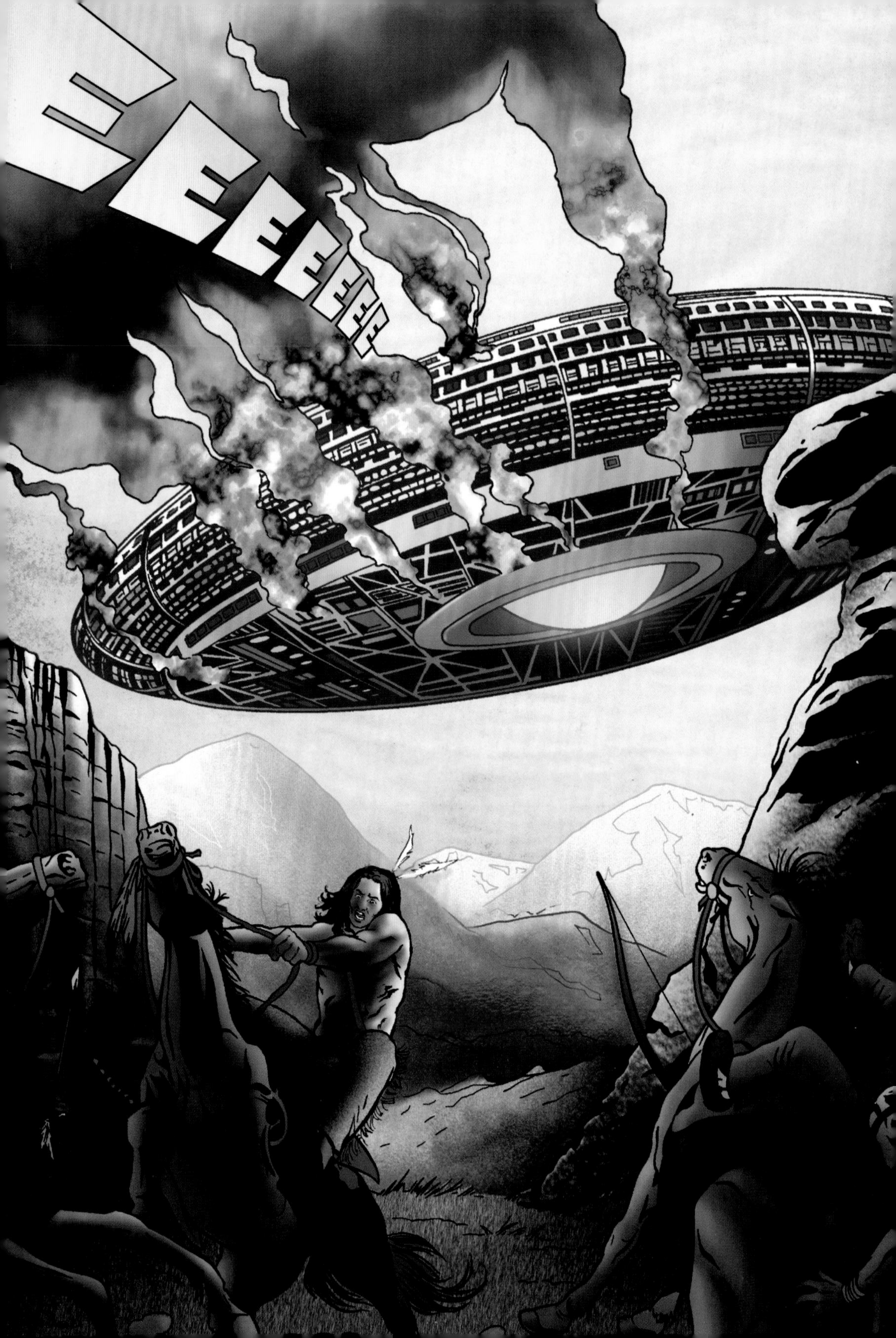
EEEEEEE

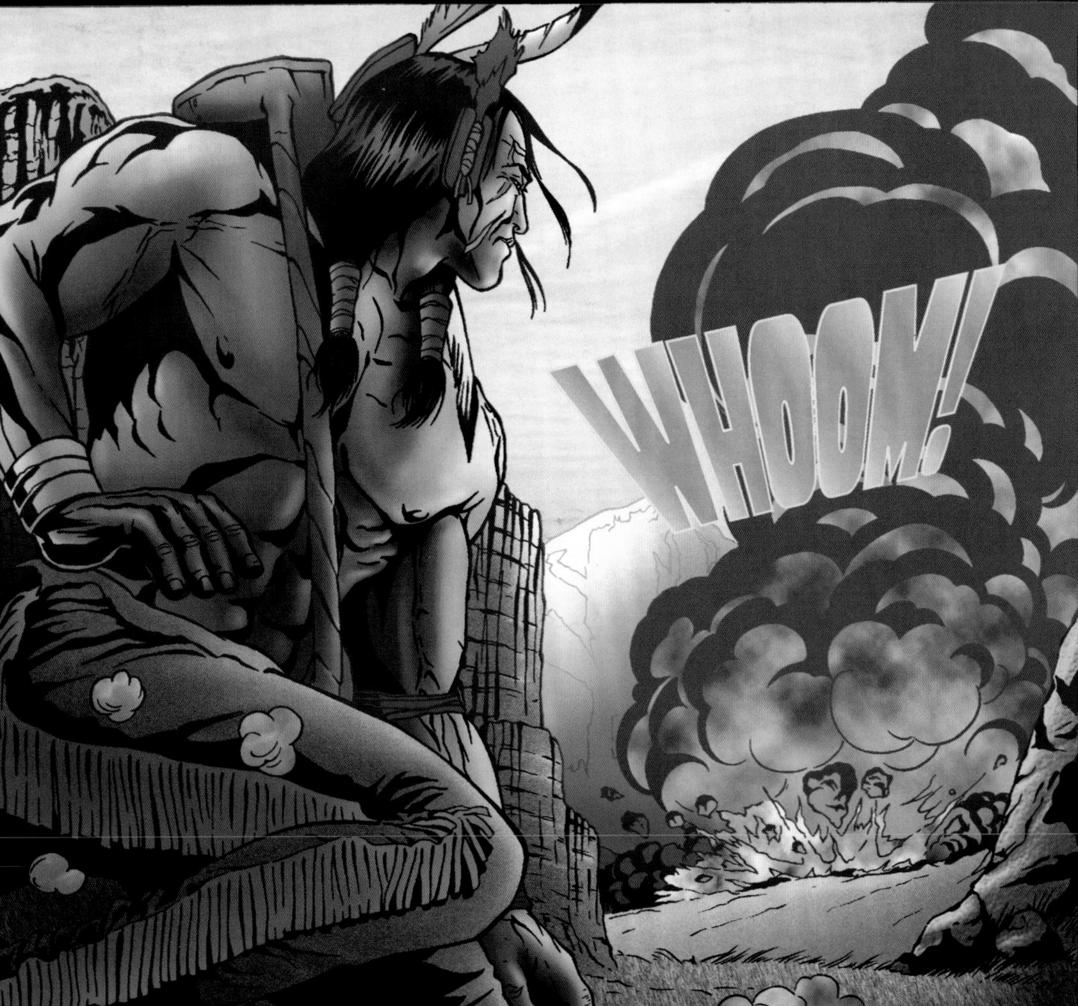
WHOOM!

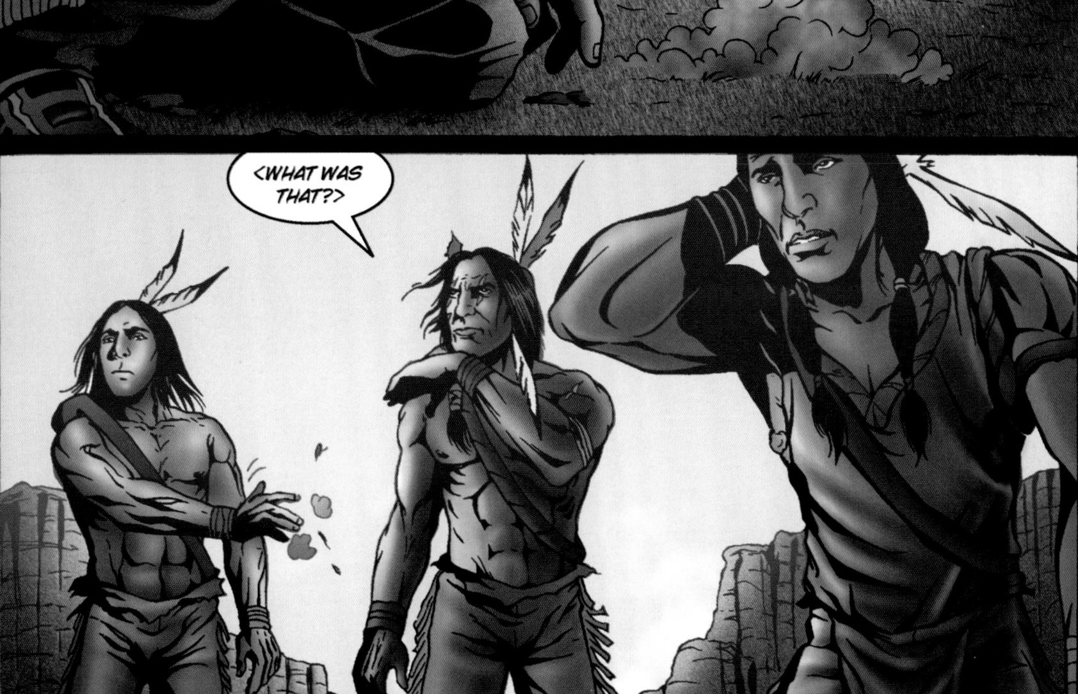
<WHAT WAS THAT?>

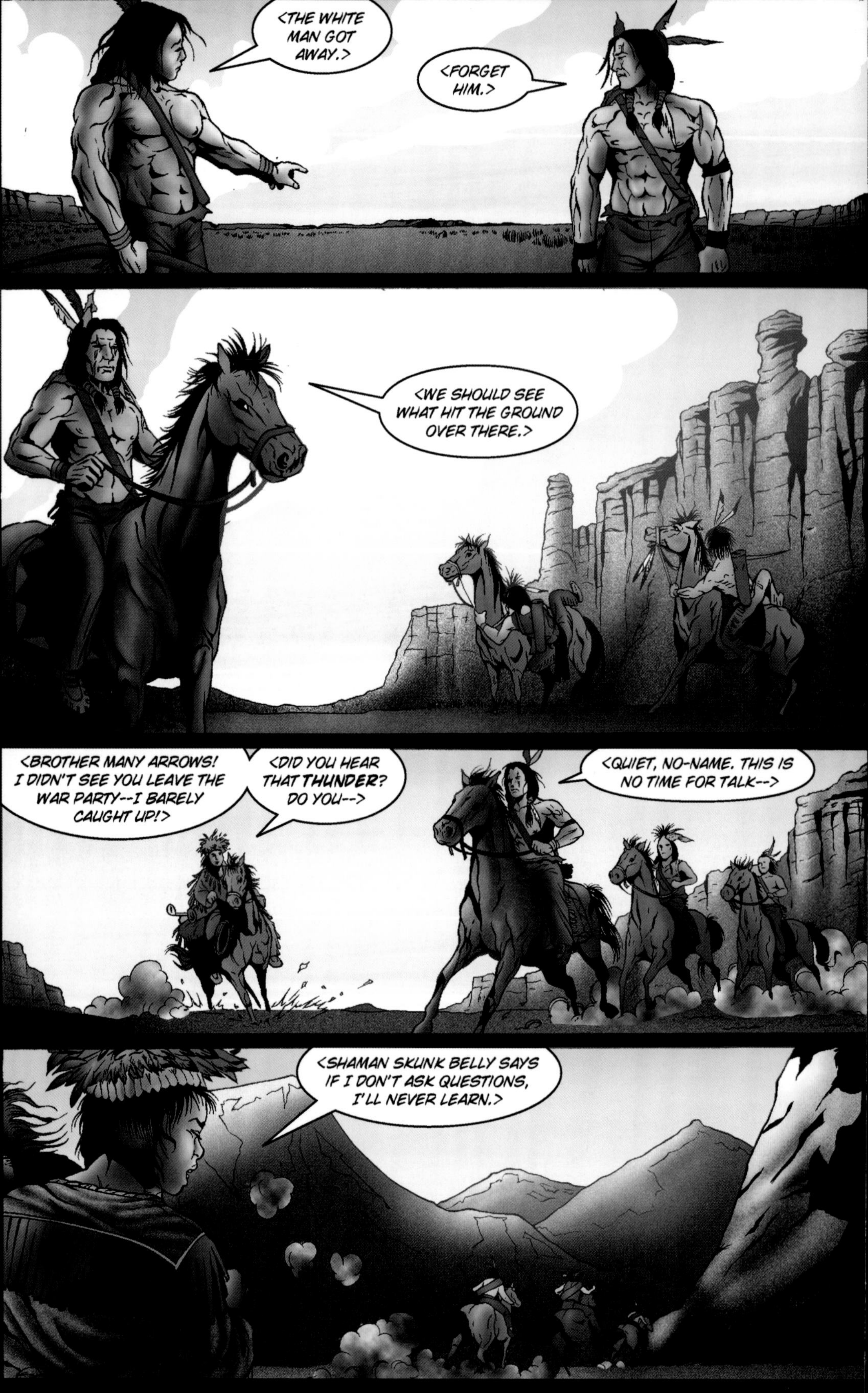
<THE WHITE MAN GOT AWAY.>
<FORGET HIM.>
<WE SHOULD SEE WHAT HIT THE GROUND OVER THERE.>
<BROTHER MANY ARROWS! I DIDN'T SEE YOU LEAVE THE WAR PARTY--I BARELY CAUGHT UP!>
<DID YOU HEAR THAT **THUNDER**? DO YOU-->
<QUIET, NO-NAME. THIS IS NO TIME FOR TALK-->
<SHAMAN SKUNK BELLY SAYS IF I DON'T ASK QUESTIONS, I'LL NEVER LEARN.>

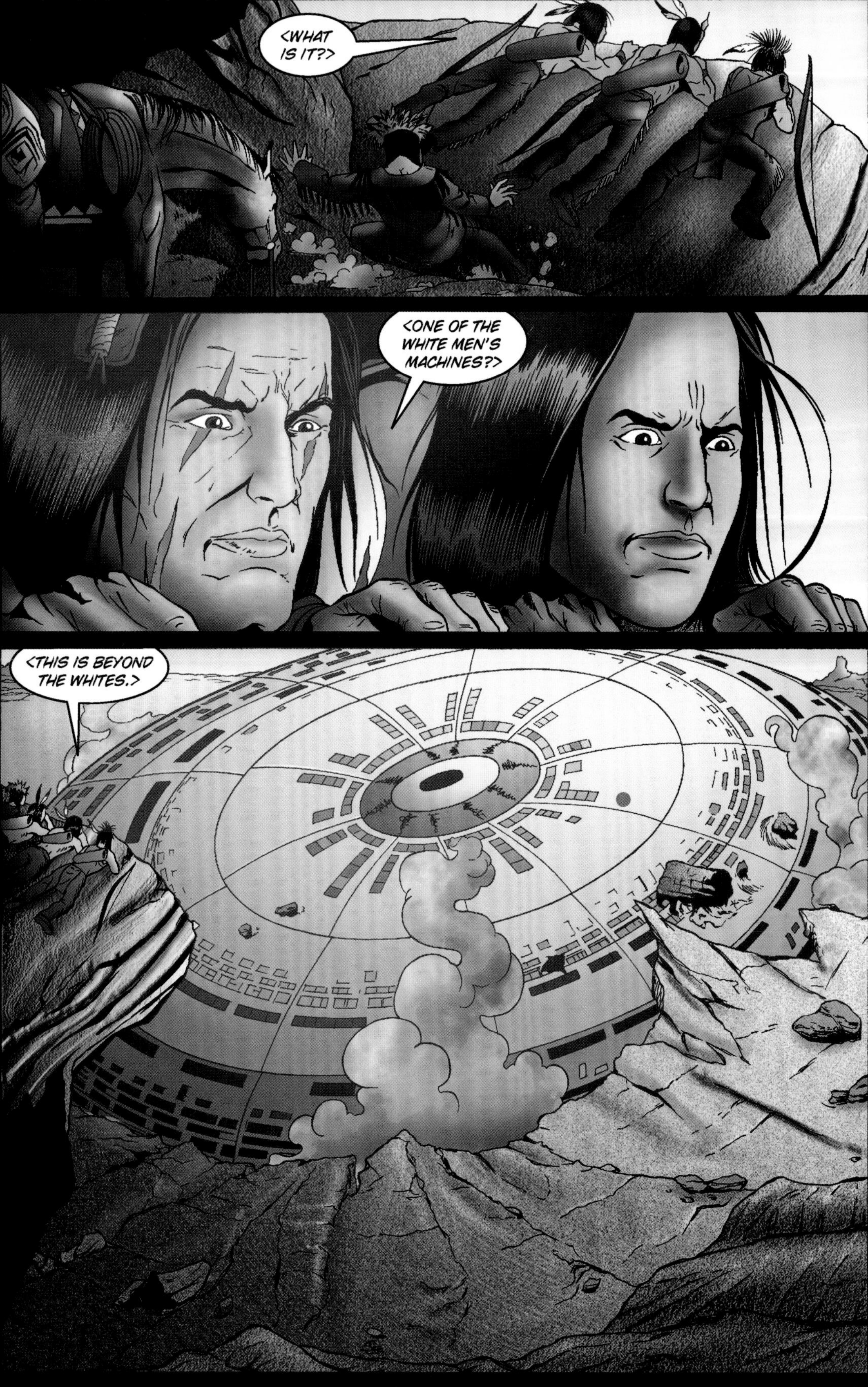
<WHAT IS IT?>
<ONE OF THE WHITE MEN'S MACHINES?>
<THIS IS BEYOND THE WHITES.>

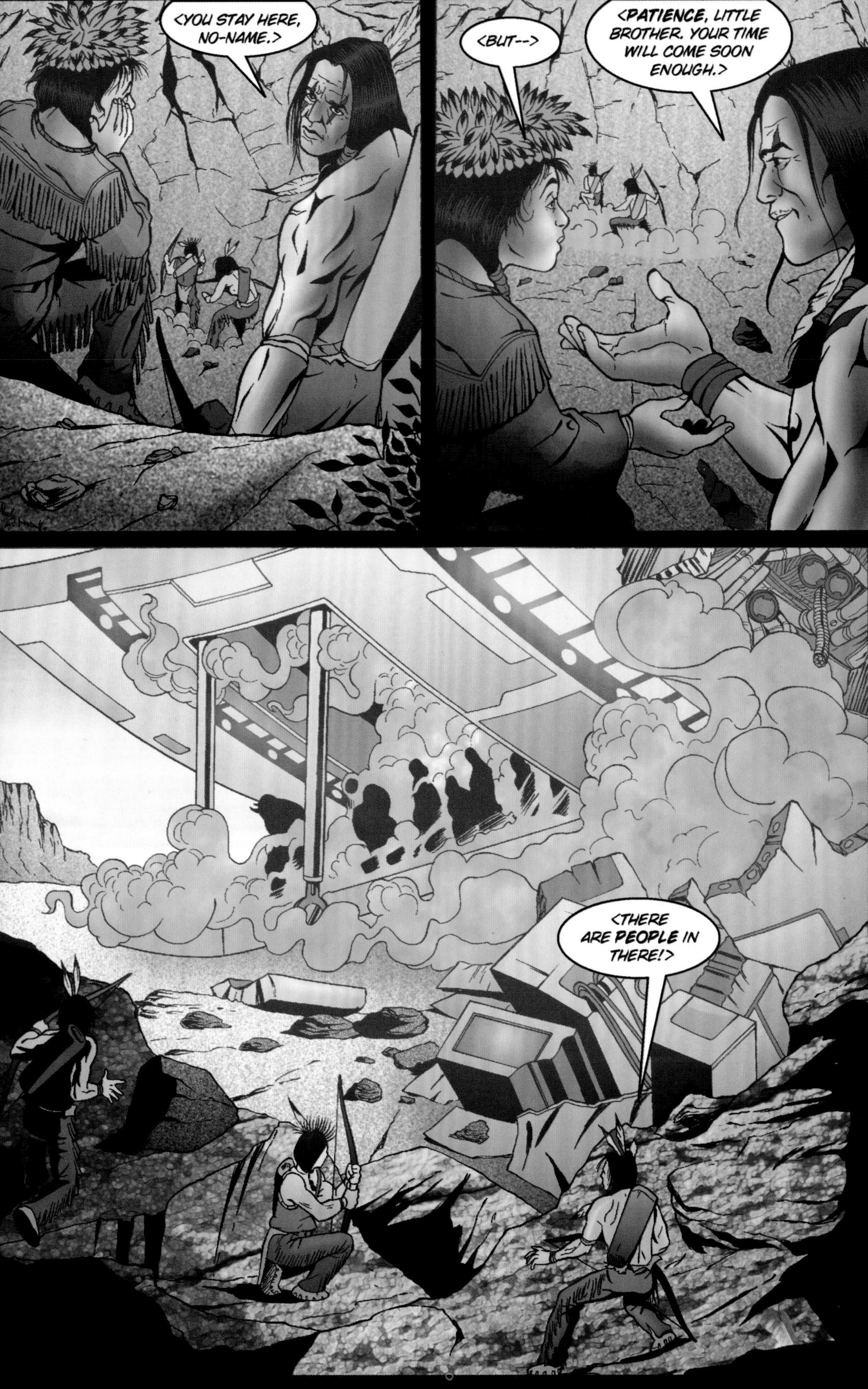
<YOU STAY HERE, NO-NAME.>
<BUT-->
<**PATIENCE**, LITTLE BROTHER. YOUR TIME WILL COME SOON ENOUGH.>
<THERE ARE **PEOPLE** IN THERE!>

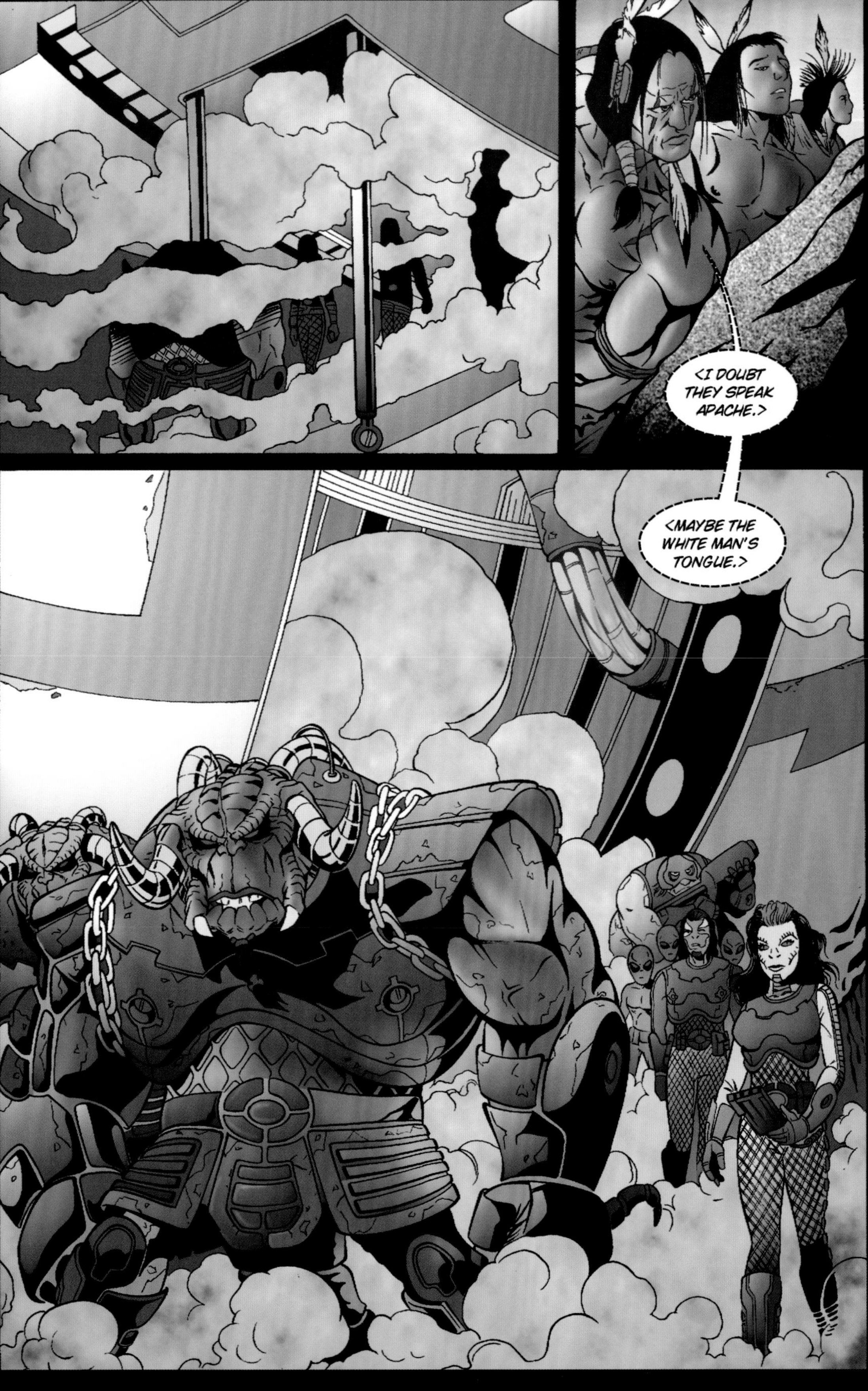
<I DOUBT THEY SPEAK APACHE.>
<MAYBE THE WHITE MAN'S TONGUE.>

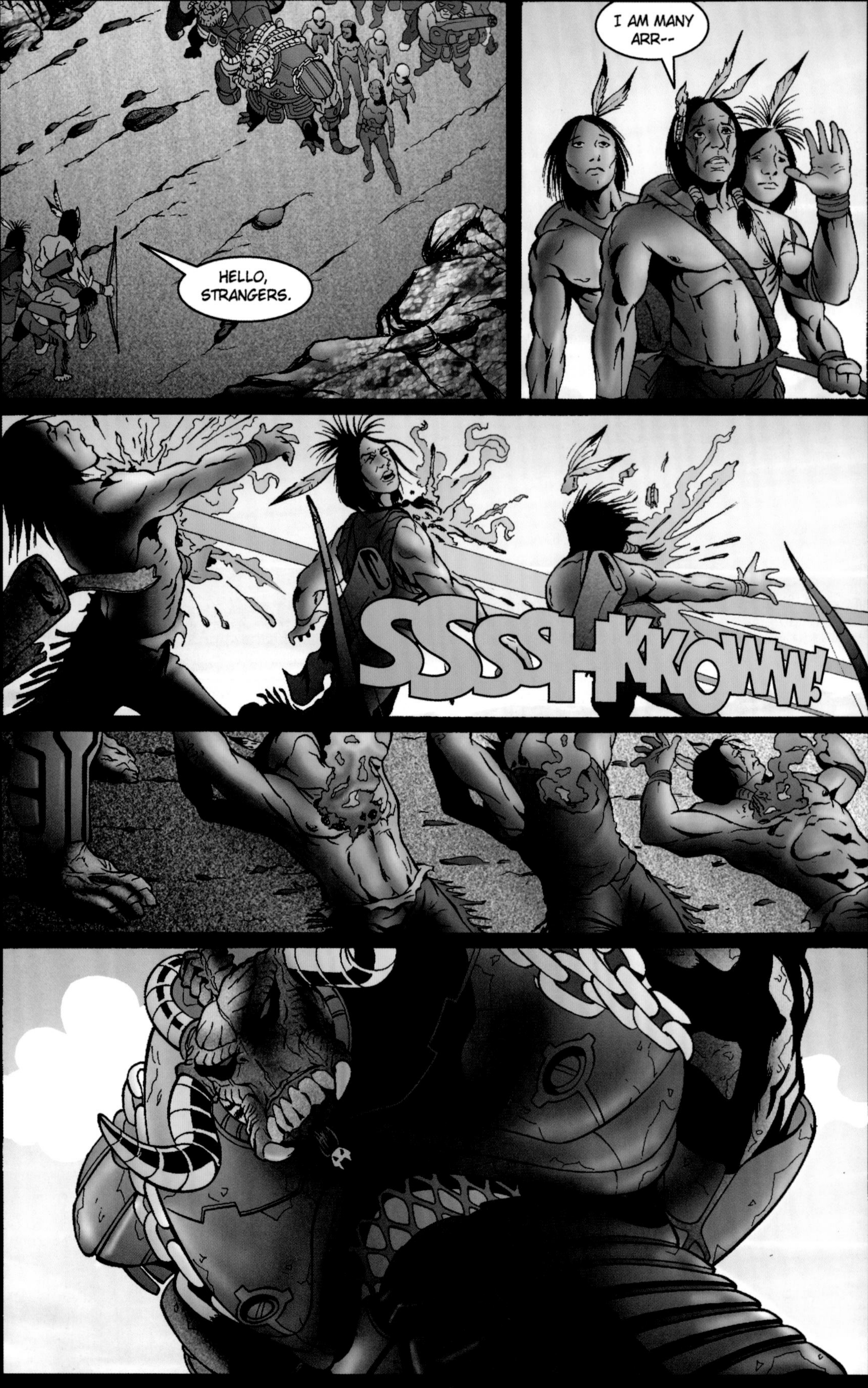
HELLO, STRANGERS.
I AM MANY ARR--
SSSHKKOWW!

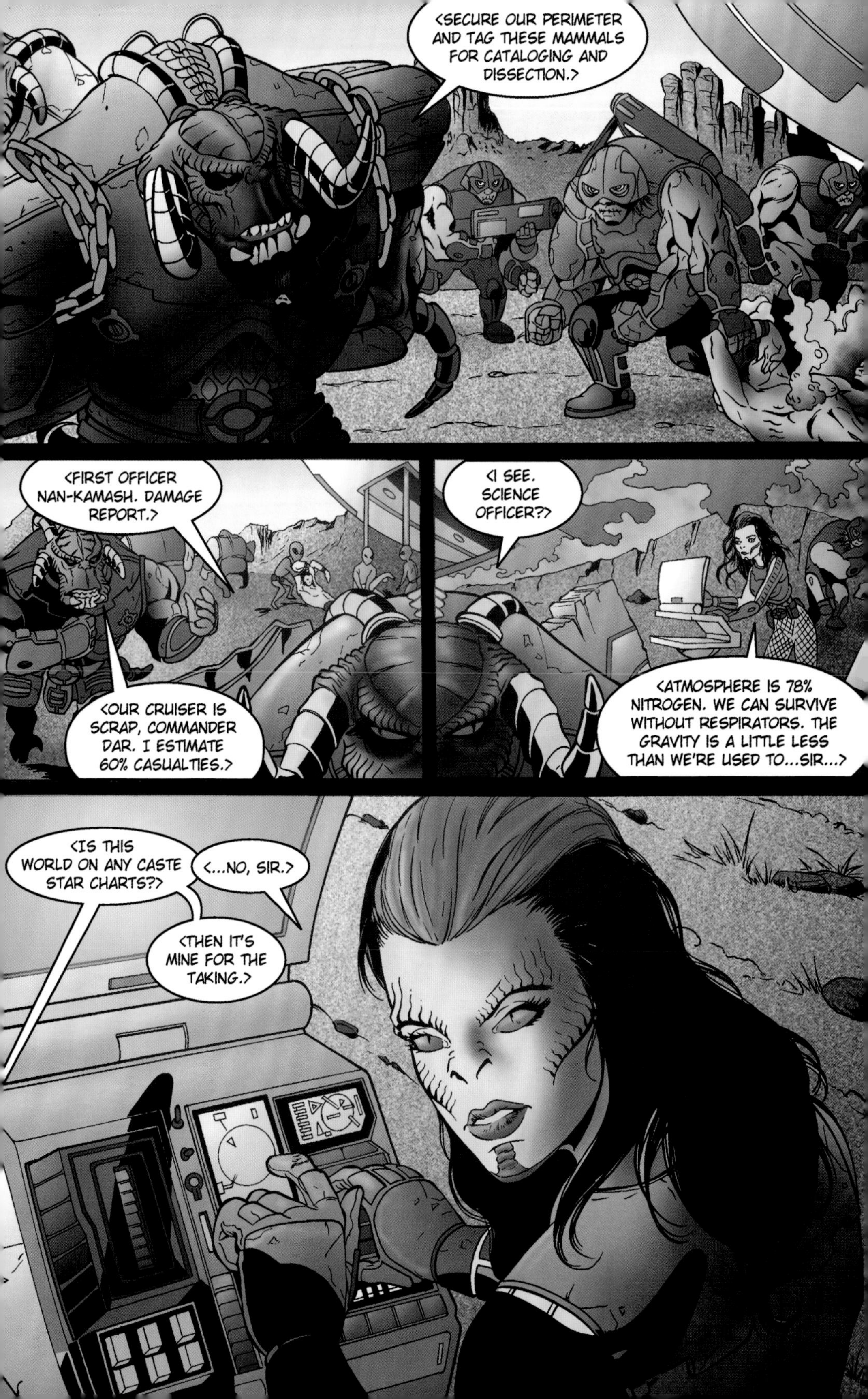
<SECURE OUR PERIMETER AND TAG THESE MAMMALS FOR CATALOGING AND DISSECTION.>
<FIRST OFFICER NAN-KAMASH. DAMAGE REPORT.>
<OUR CRUISER IS SCRAP, COMMANDER DAR. I ESTIMATE 60% CASUALTIES.>
<I SEE. SCIENCE OFFICER?>
<ATMOSPHERE IS 78% NITROGEN. WE CAN SURVIVE WITHOUT RESPIRATORS. THE GRAVITY IS A LITTLE LESS THAN WE'RE USED TO...SIR...>
<IS THIS WORLD ON ANY CASTE STAR CHARTS?>
<...NO, SIR.>
<THEN IT'S MINE FOR THE TAKING.>

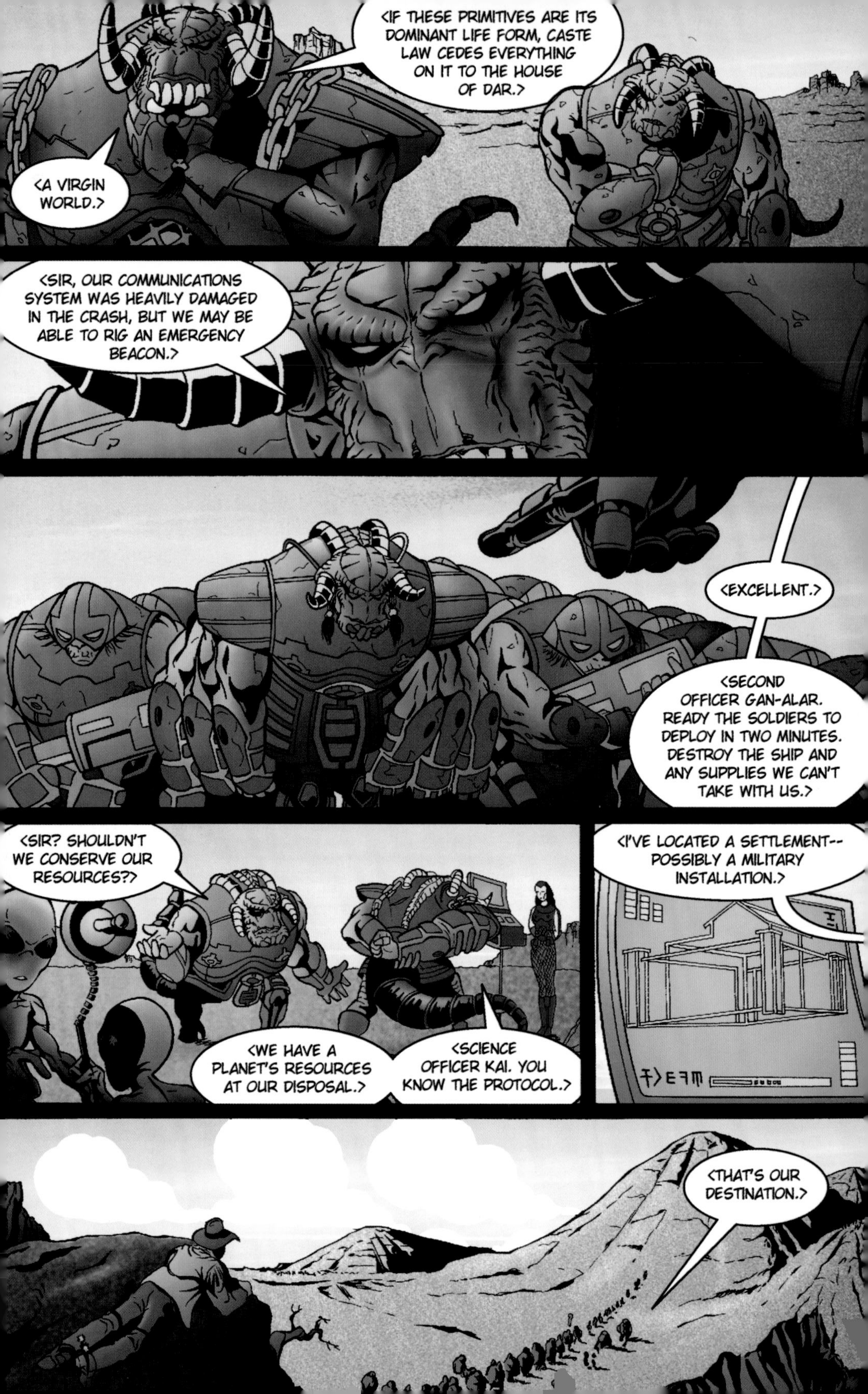
<IF THESE PRIMITIVES ARE ITS DOMINANT LIFE FORM, CASTE LAW CEDES EVERYTHING ON IT TO THE HOUSE OF DAR.>
<A VIRGIN WORLD.>
<SIR, OUR COMMUNICATIONS SYSTEM WAS HEAVILY DAMAGED IN THE CRASH, BUT WE MAY BE ABLE TO RIG AN EMERGENCY BEACON.>
<EXCELLENT.>
<SECOND OFFICER GAN-ALAR. READY THE SOLDIERS TO DEPLOY IN TWO MINUTES. DESTROY THE SHIP AND ANY SUPPLIES WE CAN'T TAKE WITH US.>
<SIR? SHOULDN'T WE CONSERVE OUR RESOURCES?>
<WE HAVE A PLANET'S RESOURCES AT OUR DISPOSAL.>
<SCIENCE OFFICER KAI. YOU KNOW THE PROTOCOL.>
<I'VE LOCATED A SETTLEMENT-- POSSIBLY A MILITARY INSTALLATION.>
<THAT'S OUR DESTINATION.>

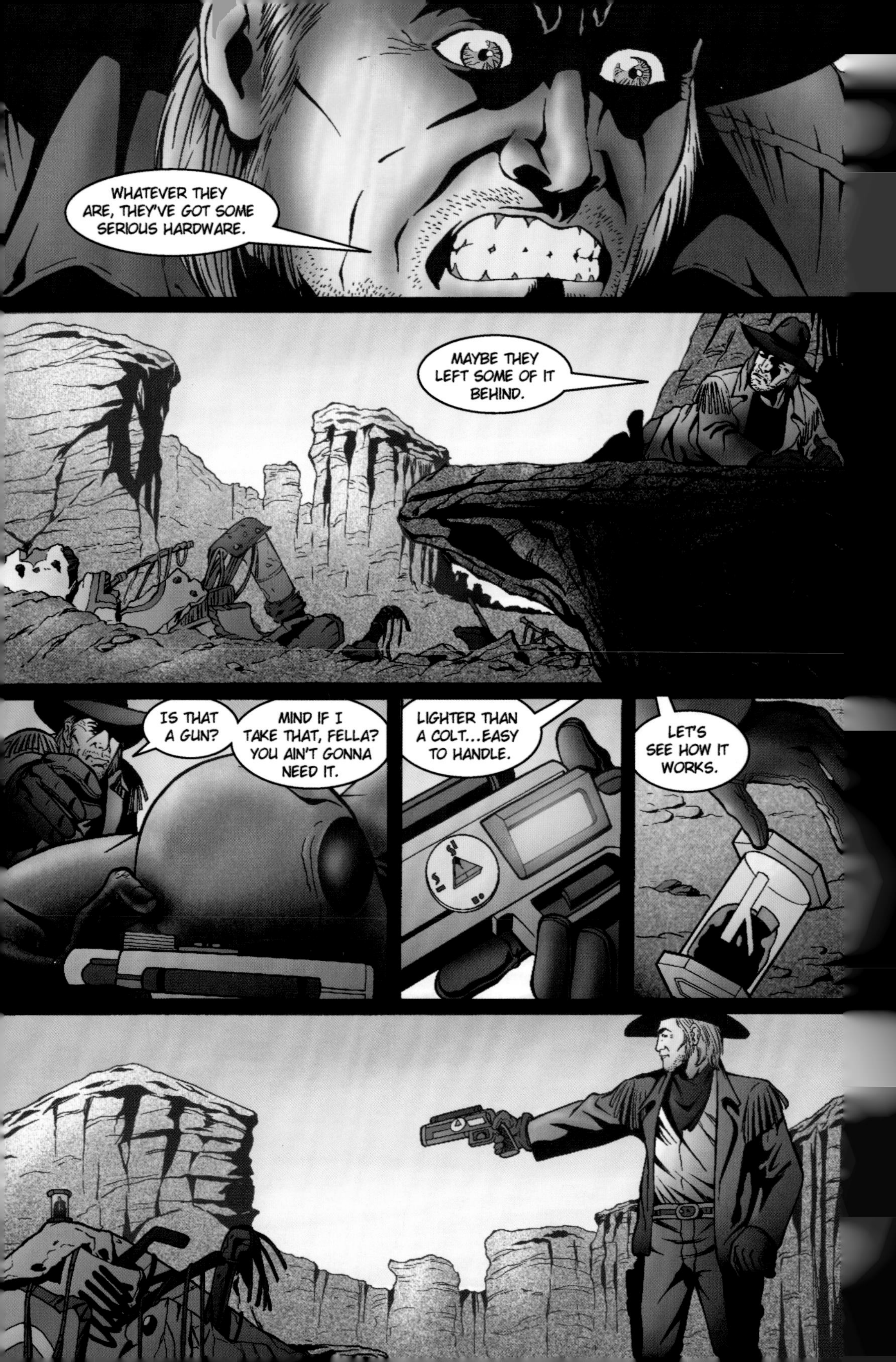
WHATEVER THEY ARE, THEY'VE GOT SOME SERIOUS HARDWARE.
MAYBE THEY LEFT SOME OF IT BEHIND.
IS THAT A GUN?
MIND IF I TAKE THAT, FELLA? YOU AIN'T GONNA NEED IT.
LIGHTER THAN A COLT...EASY TO HANDLE.
LET'S SEE HOW IT WORKS.

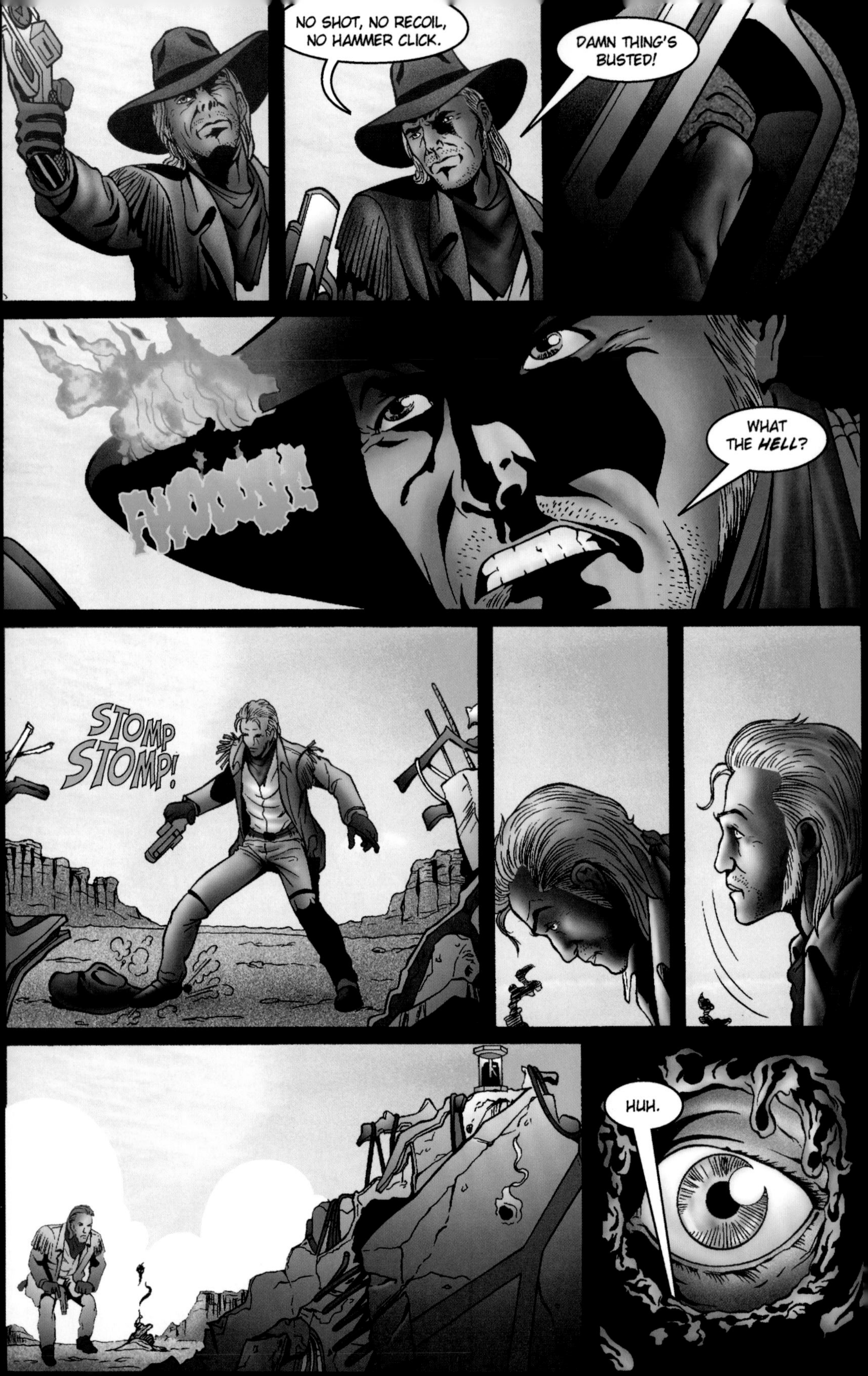
NO SHOT, NO RECOIL, NO HAMMER CLICK.
DAMN THING'S BUSTED!
FWOOSH!
WHAT THE HELL?
STOMP STOMP!
HUH.

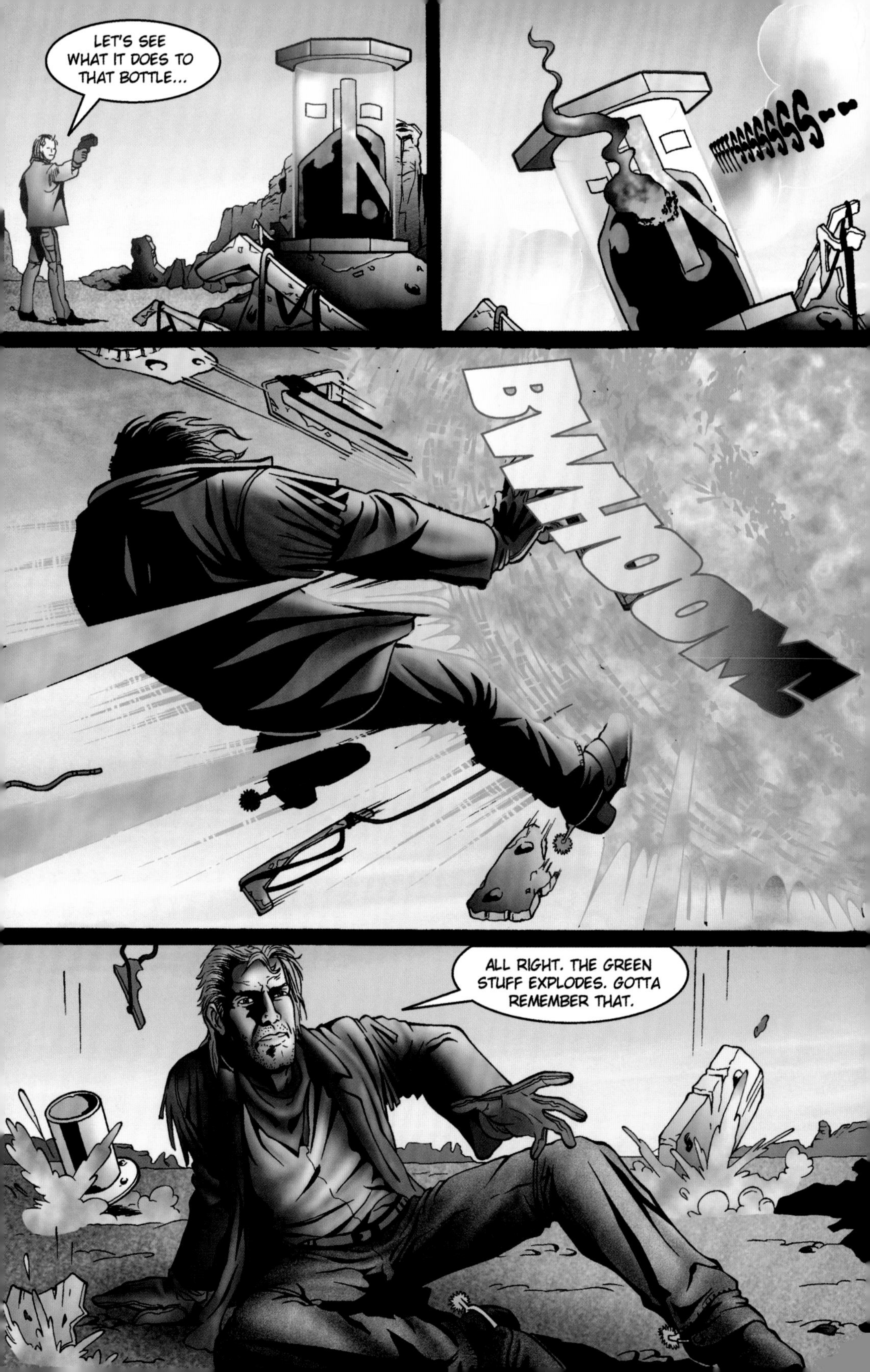
LET'S SEE WHAT IT DOES TO THAT BOTTLE...
FFFFSSSSSSSS--
BWHOOM!
ALL RIGHT. THE GREEN STUFF EXPLODES. GOTTA REMEMBER THAT.

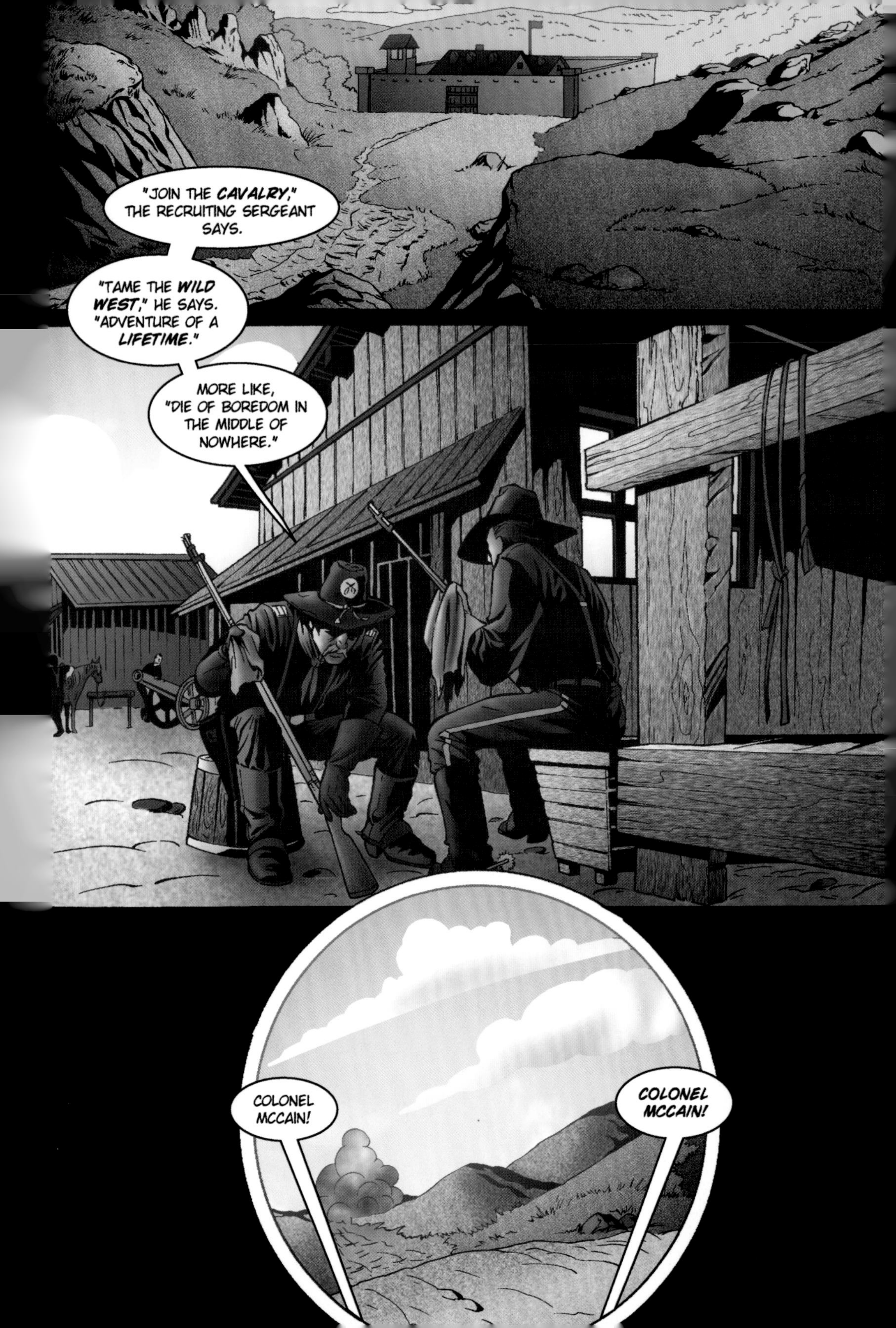
"JOIN THE **CAVALRY**," THE RECRUITING SERGEANT SAYS.
"TAME THE **WILD WEST**," HE SAYS. "ADVENTURE OF A **LIFETIME**."
MORE LIKE, "DIE OF BOREDOM IN THE MIDDLE OF NOWHERE."
COLONEL MCCAIN!
COLONEL MCCAIN!

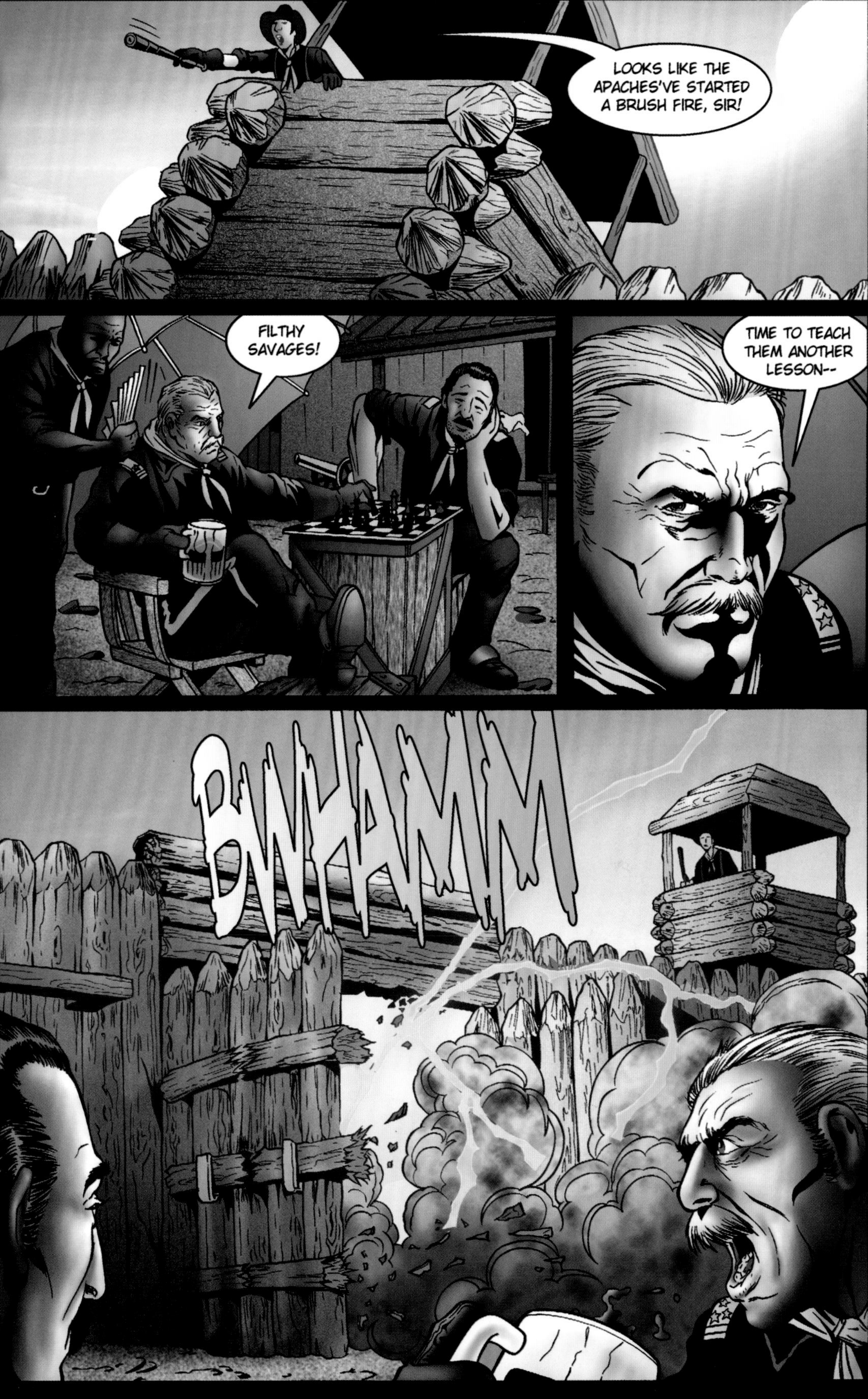
LOOKS LIKE THE APACHES'VE STARTED A BRUSH FIRE, SIR!
FILTHY SAVAGES!
TIME TO TEACH THEM ANOTHER LESSON--
BWHAMM

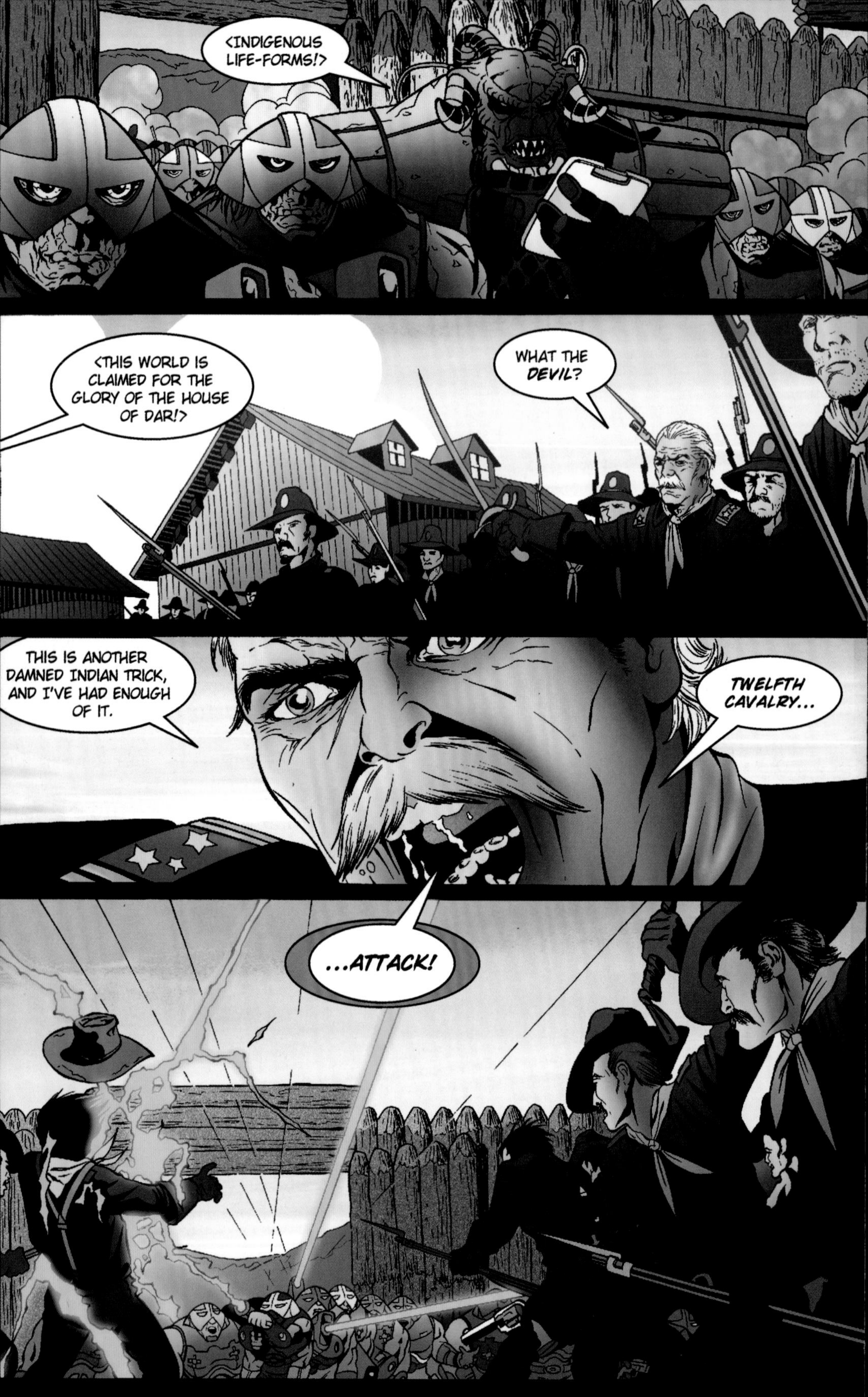
<INDIGENOUS LIFE-FORMS!>
<THIS WORLD IS CLAIMED FOR THE GLORY OF THE HOUSE OF DAR!>
WHAT THE *DEVIL*?
THIS IS ANOTHER DAMNED INDIAN TRICK, AND I'VE HAD ENOUGH OF IT.
TWELFTH CAVALRY...
...ATTACK!

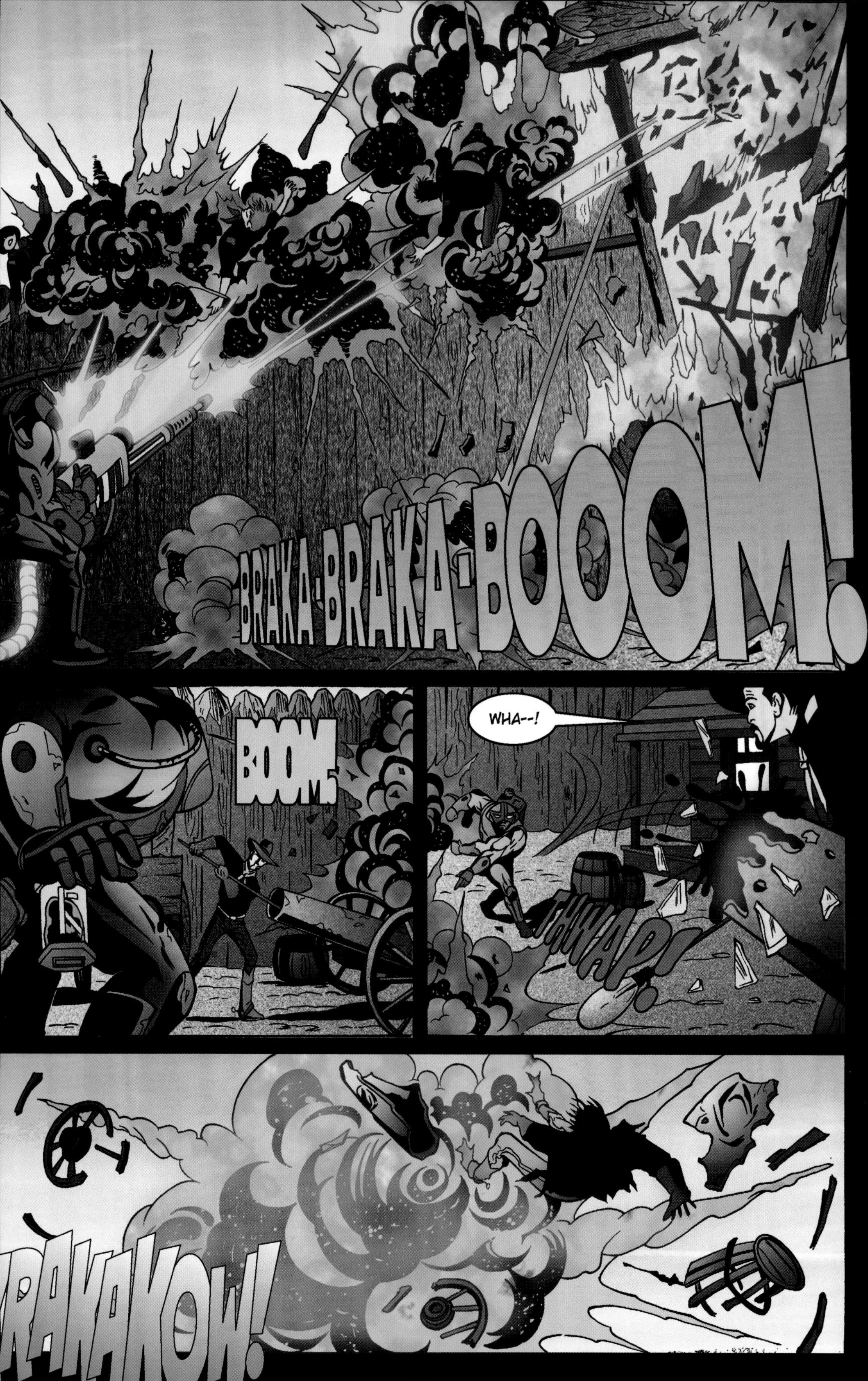
BRAKA-BRAKA-BOOOM!
BOOM.
WHA--!
THWAP!
RAKAKOW!

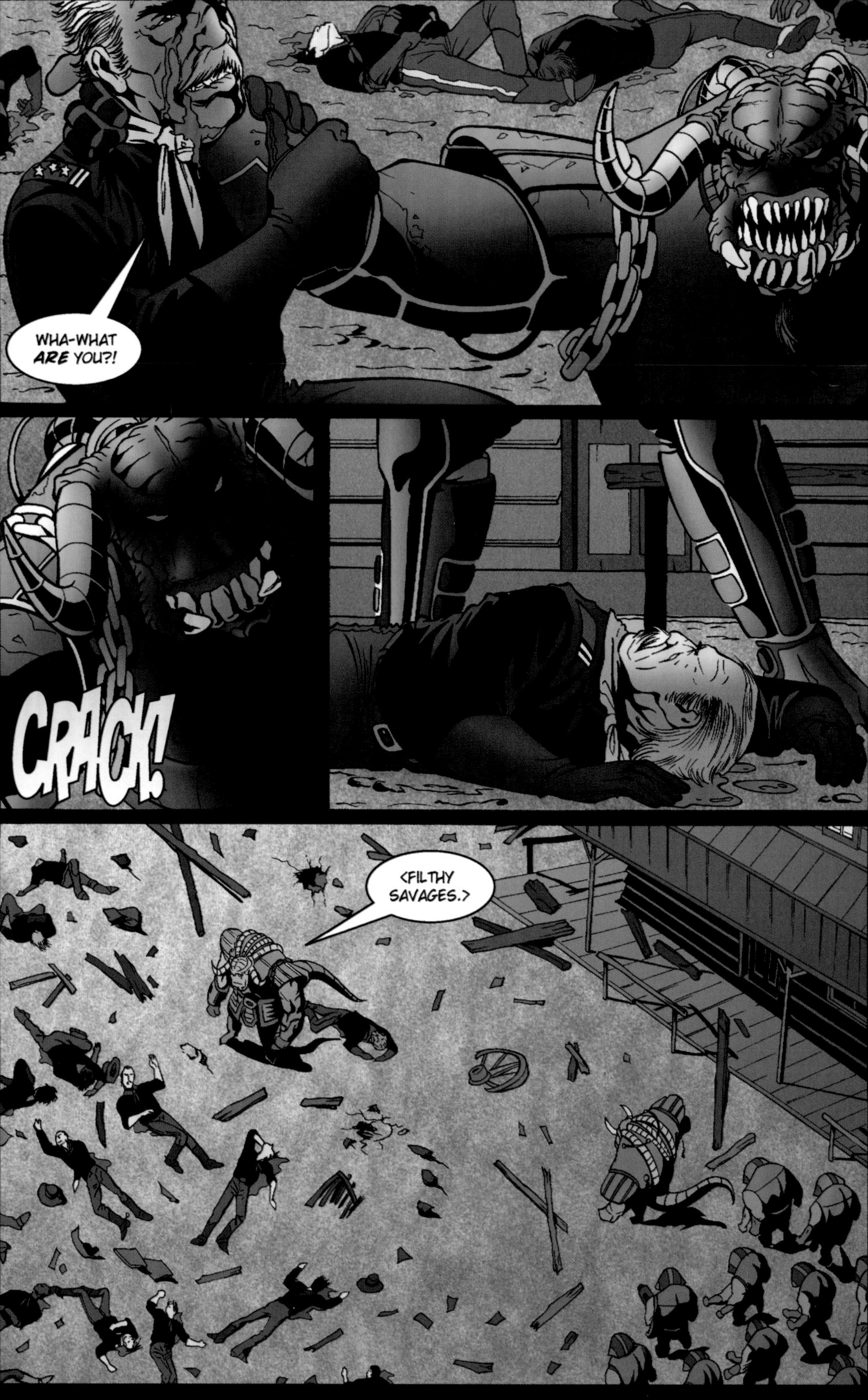
WHA-WHAT ARE YOU?!
CRACK!
<FILTHY SAVAGES.>

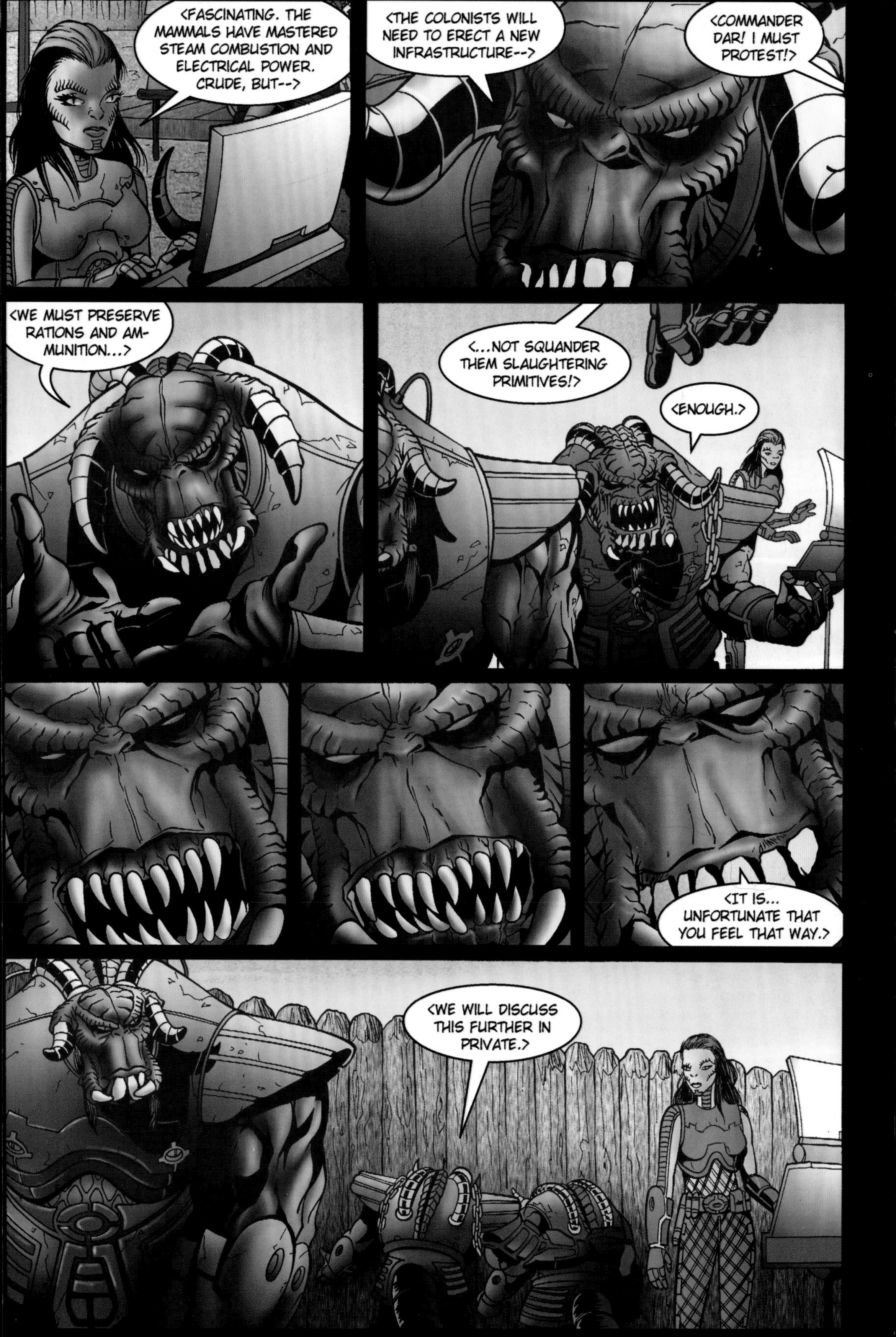
<FASCINATING. THE MAMMALS HAVE MASTERED STEAM COMBUSTION AND ELECTRICAL POWER. CRUDE, BUT-->
<THE COLONISTS WILL NEED TO ERECT A NEW INFRASTRUCTURE-->
<COMMANDER DAR! I MUST PROTEST!>
<WE MUST PRESERVE RATIONS AND AM-MUNITION...>
<...NOT SQUANDER THEM SLAUGHTERING PRIMITIVES!>
<ENOUGH.>
<IT IS... UNFORTUNATE THAT YOU FEEL THAT WAY.>
<WE WILL DISCUSS THIS FURTHER IN PRIVATE.>

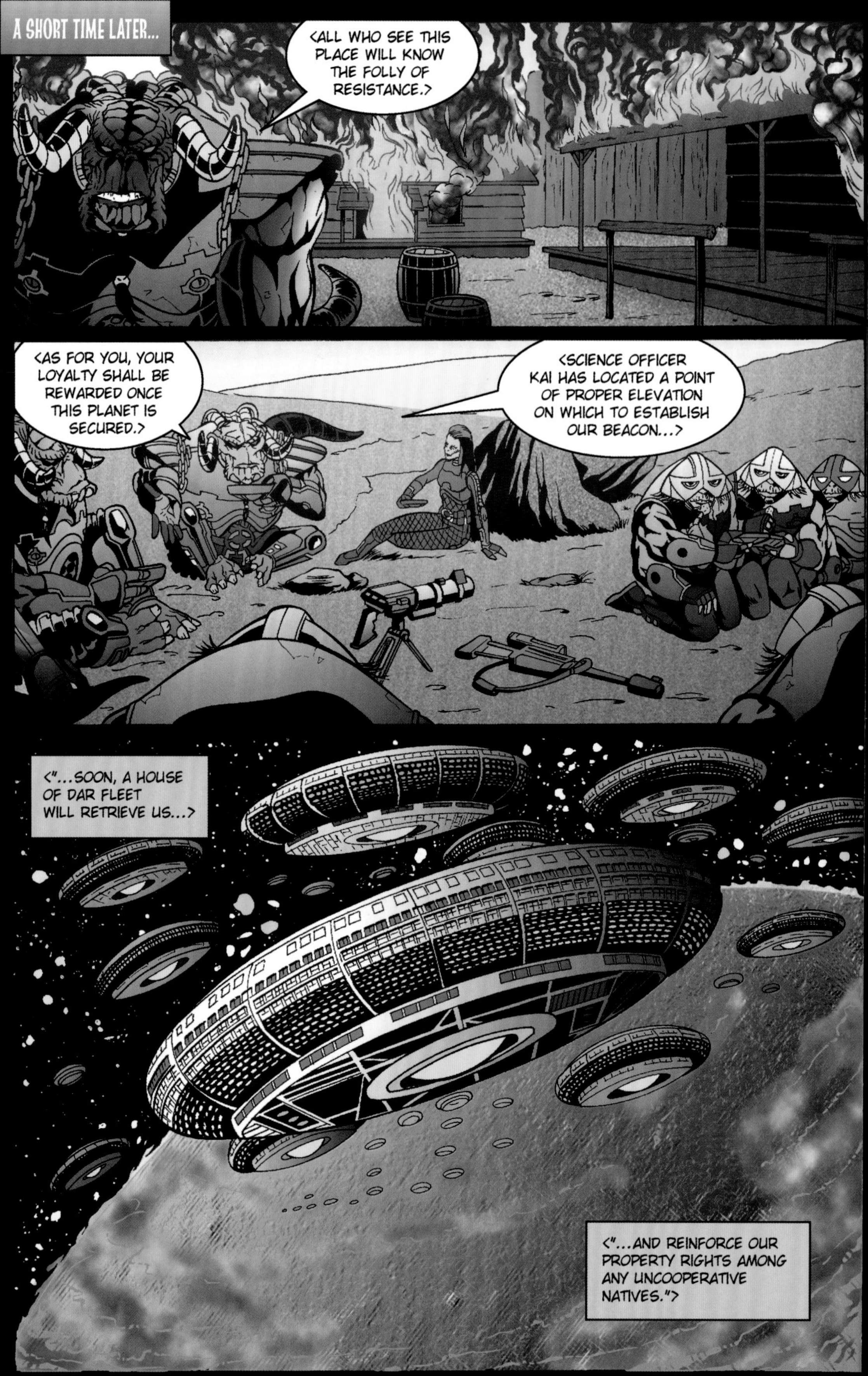
A SHORT TIME LATER...
<ALL WHO SEE THIS PLACE WILL KNOW THE FOLLY OF RESISTANCE.>
<AS FOR YOU, YOUR LOYALTY SHALL BE REWARDED ONCE THIS PLANET IS SECURED.>
<SCIENCE OFFICER KAI HAS LOCATED A POINT OF PROPER ELEVATION ON WHICH TO ESTABLISH OUR BEACON...>
<"...SOON, A HOUSE OF DAR FLEET WILL RETRIEVE US...>
<"...AND REINFORCE OUR PROPERTY RIGHTS AMONG ANY UNCOOPERATIVE NATIVES.">

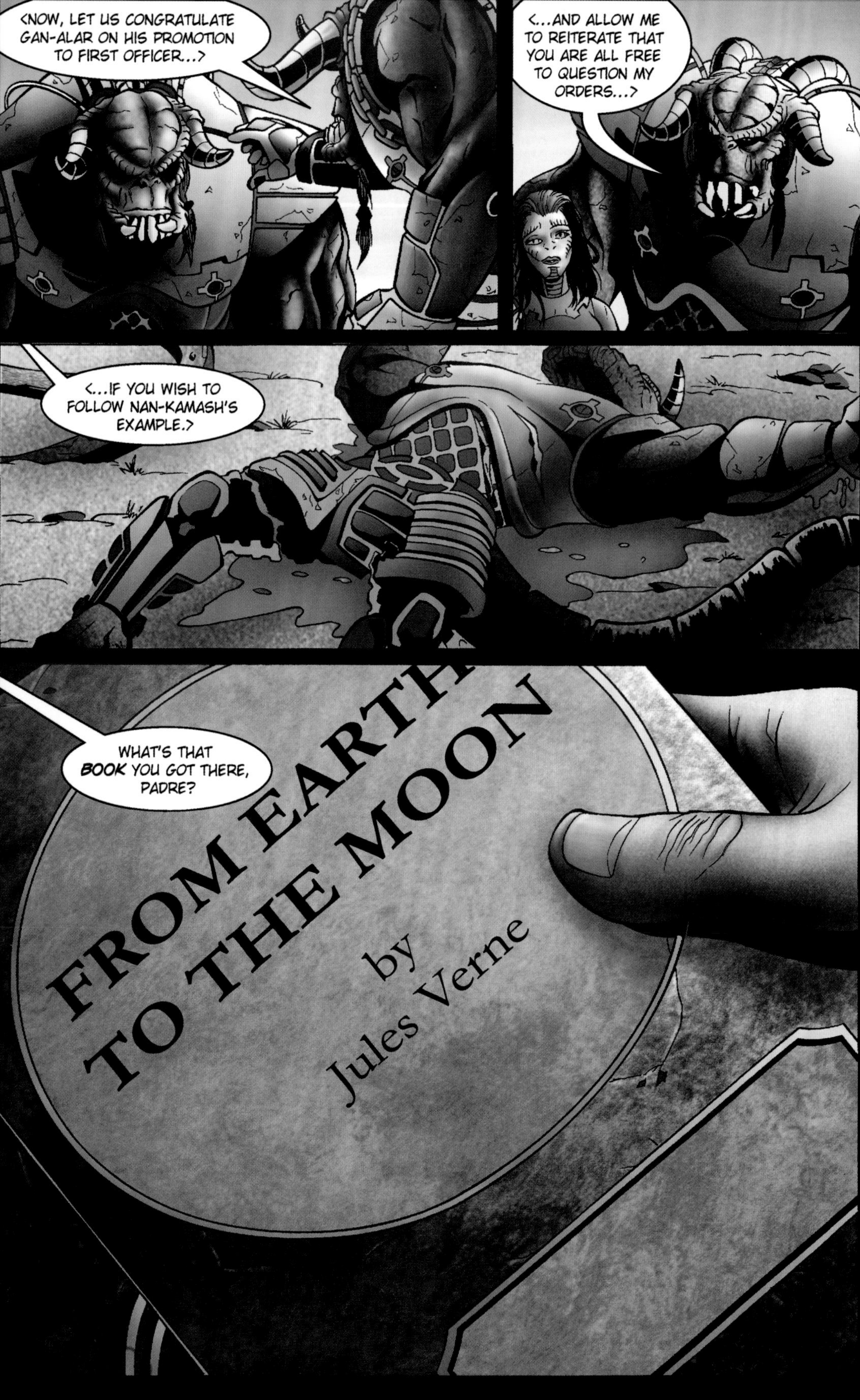
<NOW, LET US CONGRATULATE GAN-ALAR ON HIS PROMOTION TO FIRST OFFICER...>
<...AND ALLOW ME TO REITERATE THAT YOU ARE ALL FREE TO QUESTION MY ORDERS...>
<...IF YOU WISH TO FOLLOW NAN-KAMASH'S EXAMPLE.>
WHAT'S THAT **BOOK** YOU GOT THERE, PADRE?
FROM EARTH TO THE MOON
by
Jules Verne

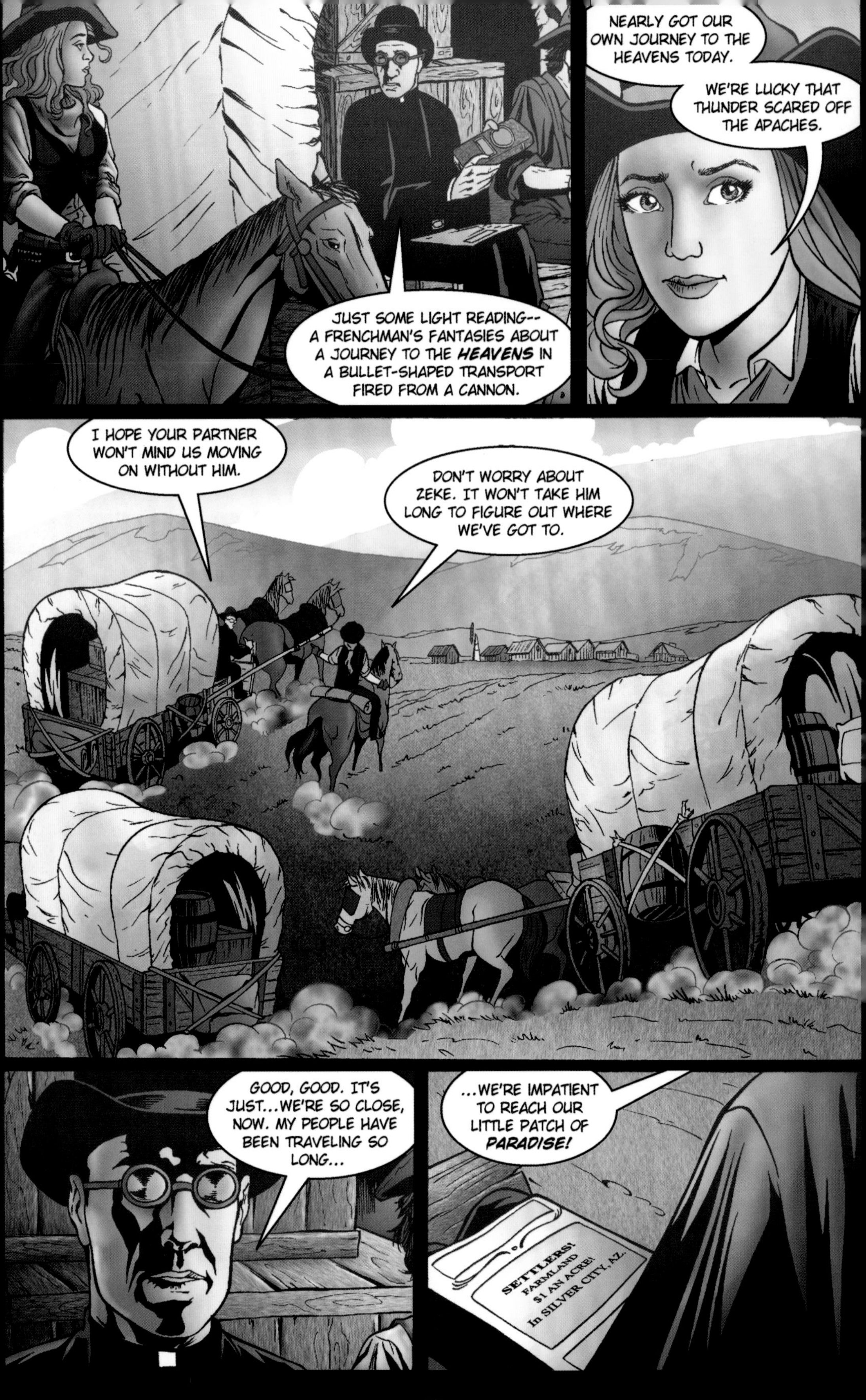
JUST SOME LIGHT READING--A FRENCHMAN'S FANTASIES ABOUT A JOURNEY TO THE *HEAVENS* IN A BULLET-SHAPED TRANSPORT FIRED FROM A CANNON.
NEARLY GOT OUR OWN JOURNEY TO THE HEAVENS TODAY.
WE'RE LUCKY THAT THUNDER SCARED OFF THE APACHES.
I HOPE YOUR PARTNER WON'T MIND US MOVING ON WITHOUT HIM.
DON'T WORRY ABOUT ZEKE. IT WON'T TAKE HIM LONG TO FIGURE OUT WHERE WE'VE GOT TO.
GOOD, GOOD. IT'S JUST...WE'RE SO CLOSE, NOW. MY PEOPLE HAVE BEEN TRAVELING SO LONG...
...WE'RE IMPATIENT TO REACH OUR LITTLE PATCH OF *PARADISE!*
SETTLERS!
FARMLAND
$1 AN ACRE!
In SILVER CITY, AZ.

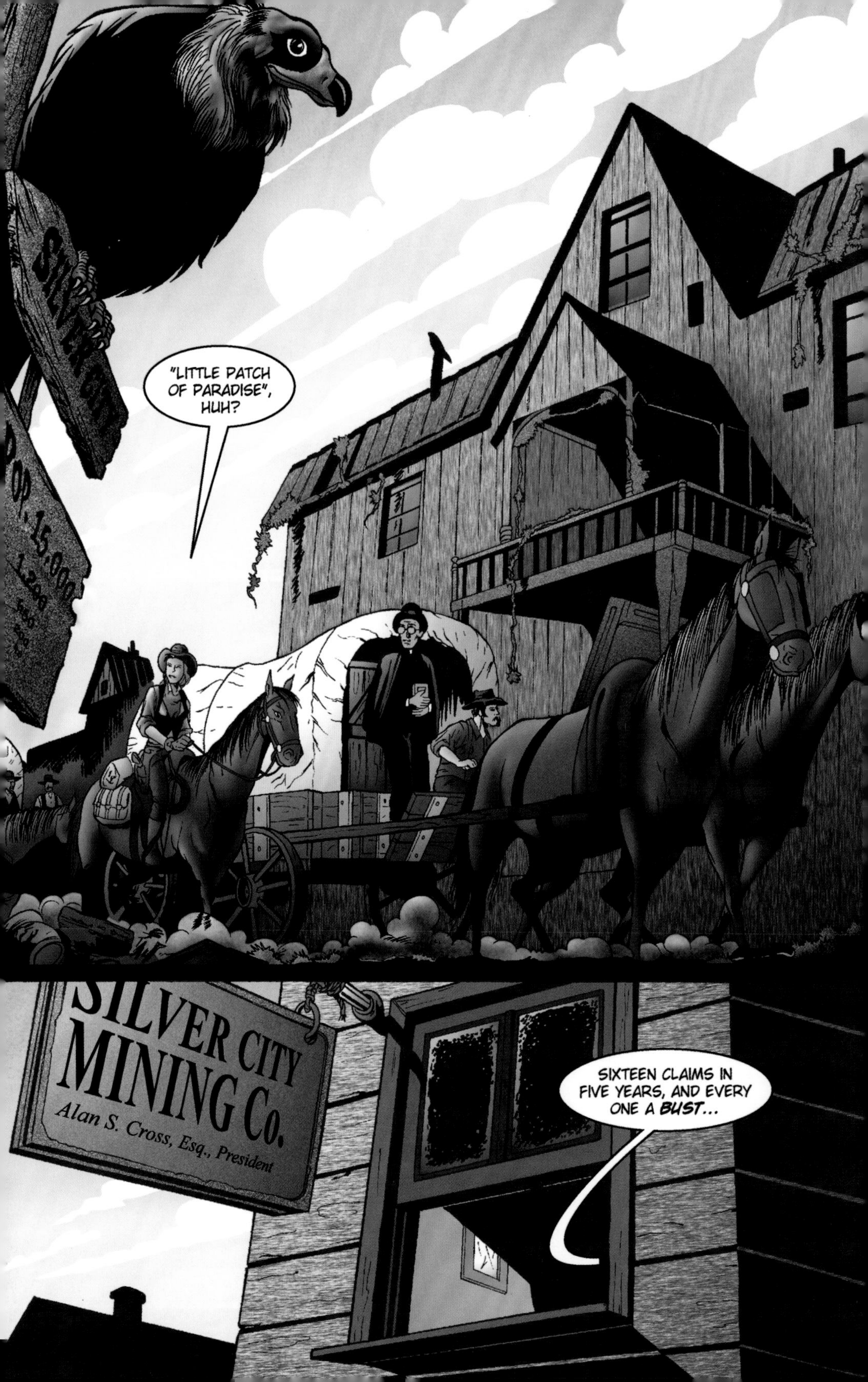
"LITTLE PATCH OF PARADISE", HUH?
SILVER CITY MINING Co.
Alan S. Cross, Esq., President
SIXTEEN CLAIMS IN FIVE YEARS, AND EVERY ONE A BUST...

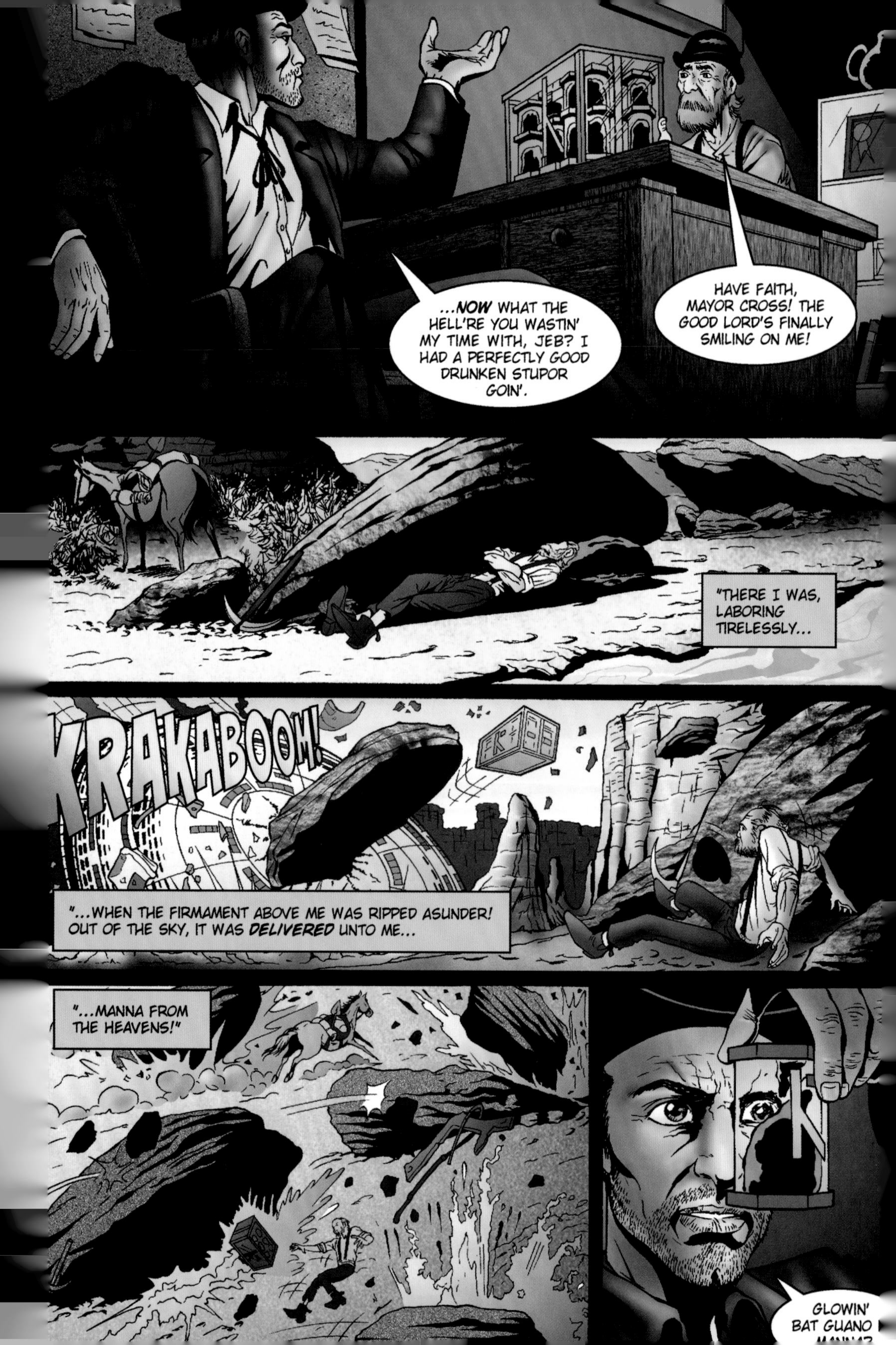
...NOW WHAT THE HELL'RE YOU WASTIN' MY TIME WITH, JEB? I HAD A PERFECTLY GOOD DRUNKEN STUPOR GOIN'.
HAVE FAITH, MAYOR CROSS! THE GOOD LORD'S FINALLY SMILING ON ME!
"THERE I WAS, LABORING TIRELESSLY...
KRAKABOOM!
"...WHEN THE FIRMAMENT ABOVE ME WAS RIPPED ASUNDER! OUT OF THE SKY, IT WAS DELIVERED UNTO ME...
"...MANNA FROM THE HEAVENS!"
GLOWIN' BAT GUANO

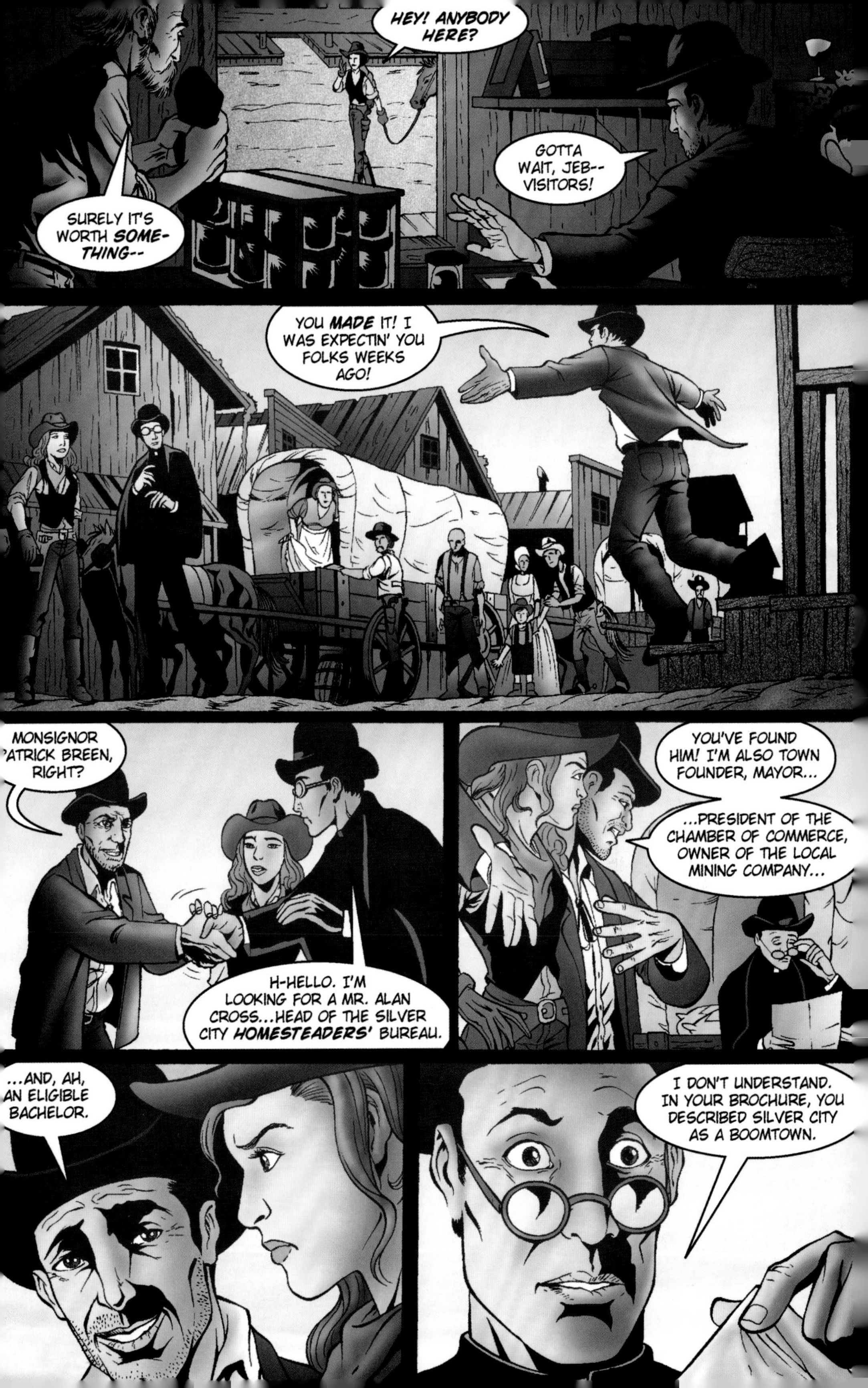
HEY! ANYBODY HERE?
SURELY IT'S WORTH SOME-THING--
GOTTA WAIT, JEB--VISITORS!
YOU MADE IT! I WAS EXPECTIN' YOU FOLKS WEEKS AGO!
MONSIGNOR PATRICK BREEN, RIGHT?
H-HELLO. I'M LOOKING FOR A MR. ALAN CROSS...HEAD OF THE SILVER CITY HOMESTEADERS' BUREAU.
YOU'VE FOUND HIM! I'M ALSO TOWN FOUNDER, MAYOR...
...PRESIDENT OF THE CHAMBER OF COMMERCE, OWNER OF THE LOCAL MINING COMPANY...
...AND, AH, AN ELIGIBLE BACHELOR.
I DON'T UNDERSTAND. IN YOUR BROCHURE, YOU DESCRIBED SILVER CITY AS A BOOMTOWN.

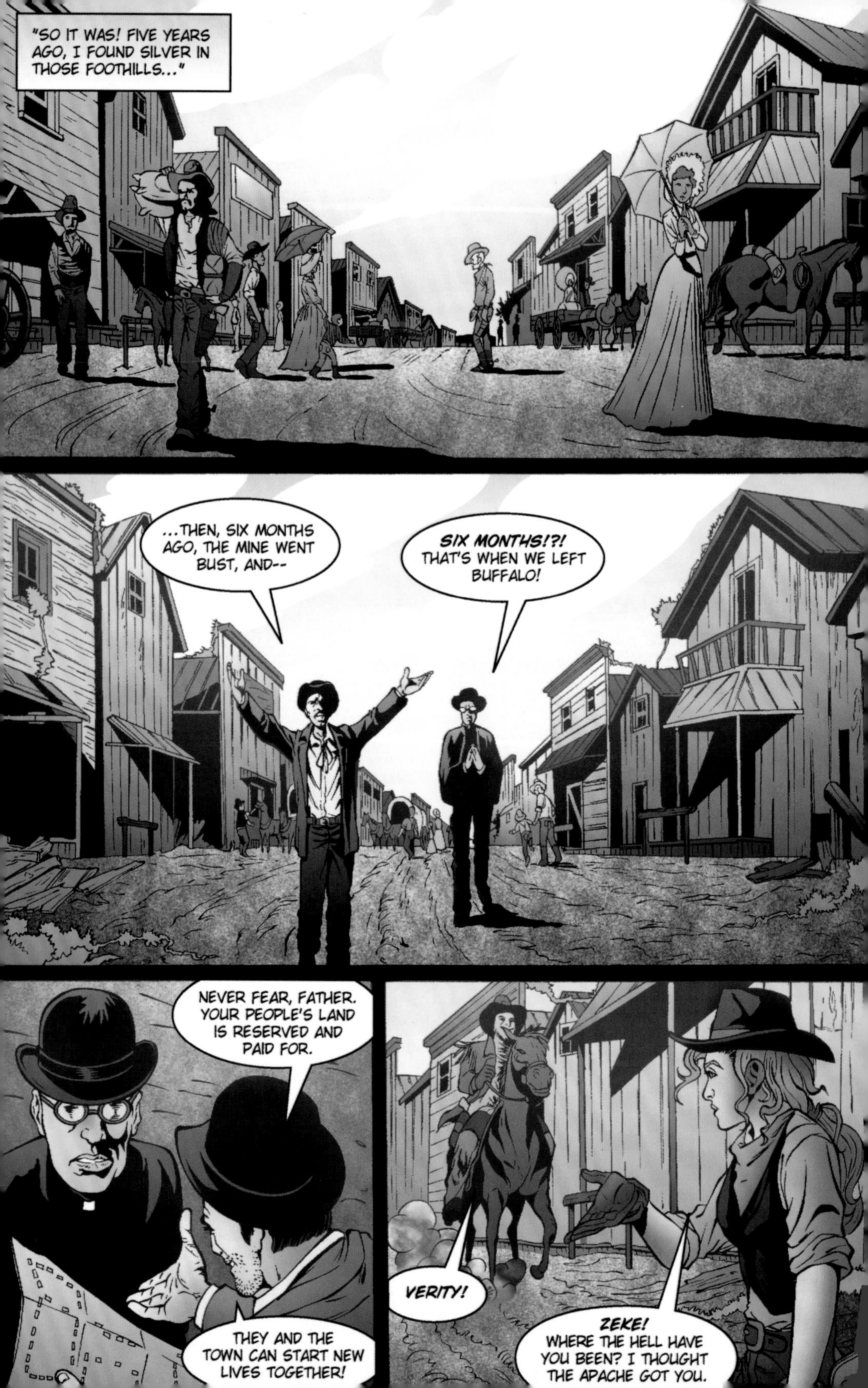
"SO IT WAS! FIVE YEARS AGO, I FOUND SILVER IN THOSE FOOTHILLS..."
...THEN, SIX MONTHS AGO, THE MINE WENT BUST, AND--
SIX MONTHS!?! THAT'S WHEN WE LEFT BUFFALO!
NEVER FEAR, FATHER. YOUR PEOPLE'S LAND IS RESERVED AND PAID FOR.
THEY AND THE TOWN CAN START NEW LIVES TOGETHER!
VERITY!
ZEKE! WHERE THE HELL HAVE YOU BEEN? I THOUGHT THE APACHE GOT YOU.

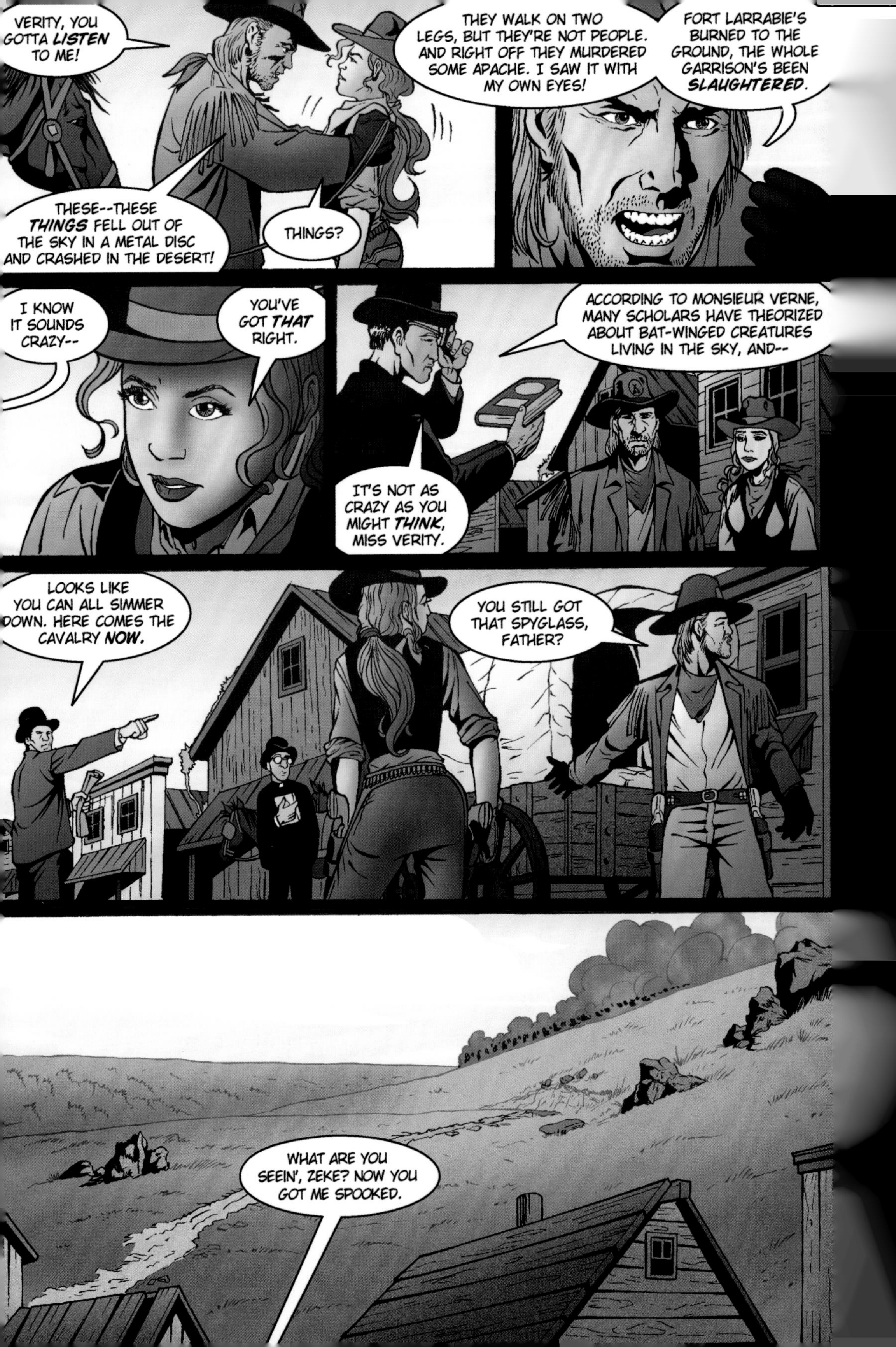
VERITY, YOU GOTTA **LISTEN** TO ME!
THESE--THESE **THINGS** FELL OUT OF THE SKY IN A METAL DISC AND CRASHED IN THE DESERT!
THINGS?
THEY WALK ON TWO LEGS, BUT THEY'RE NOT PEOPLE. AND RIGHT OFF THEY MURDERED SOME APACHE. I SAW IT WITH MY OWN EYES!
FORT LARRABIE'S BURNED TO THE GROUND, THE WHOLE GARRISON'S BEEN **SLAUGHTERED**.
I KNOW IT SOUNDS CRAZY--
YOU'VE GOT **THAT** RIGHT.
ACCORDING TO MONSIEUR VERNE, MANY SCHOLARS HAVE THEORIZED ABOUT BAT-WINGED CREATURES LIVING IN THE SKY, AND--
IT'S NOT AS CRAZY AS YOU MIGHT **THINK**, MISS VERITY.
LOOKS LIKE YOU CAN ALL SIMMER DOWN. HERE COMES THE CAVALRY **NOW.**
YOU STILL GOT THAT SPYGLASS, FATHER?
WHAT ARE YOU SEEIN', ZEKE? NOW YOU GOT ME SPOOKED.

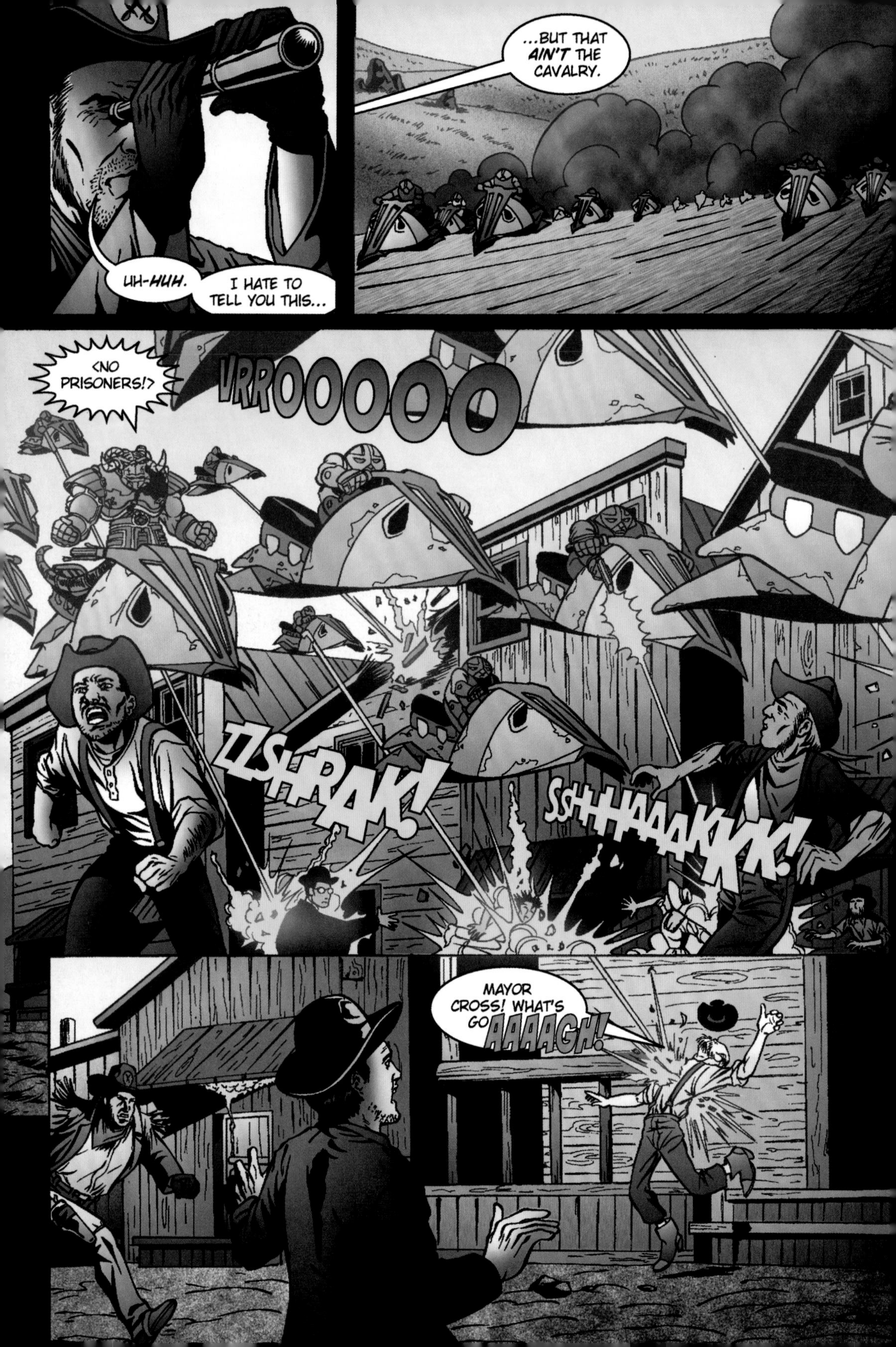
UH-HUH.
I HATE TO TELL YOU THIS...
...BUT THAT AIN'T THE CAVALRY.
<NO PRISONERS!>
VRROOOOOO
TZSHRAK!
SSHHAAAKKKK!
MAYOR CROSS! WHAT'S GO AAAAGH!

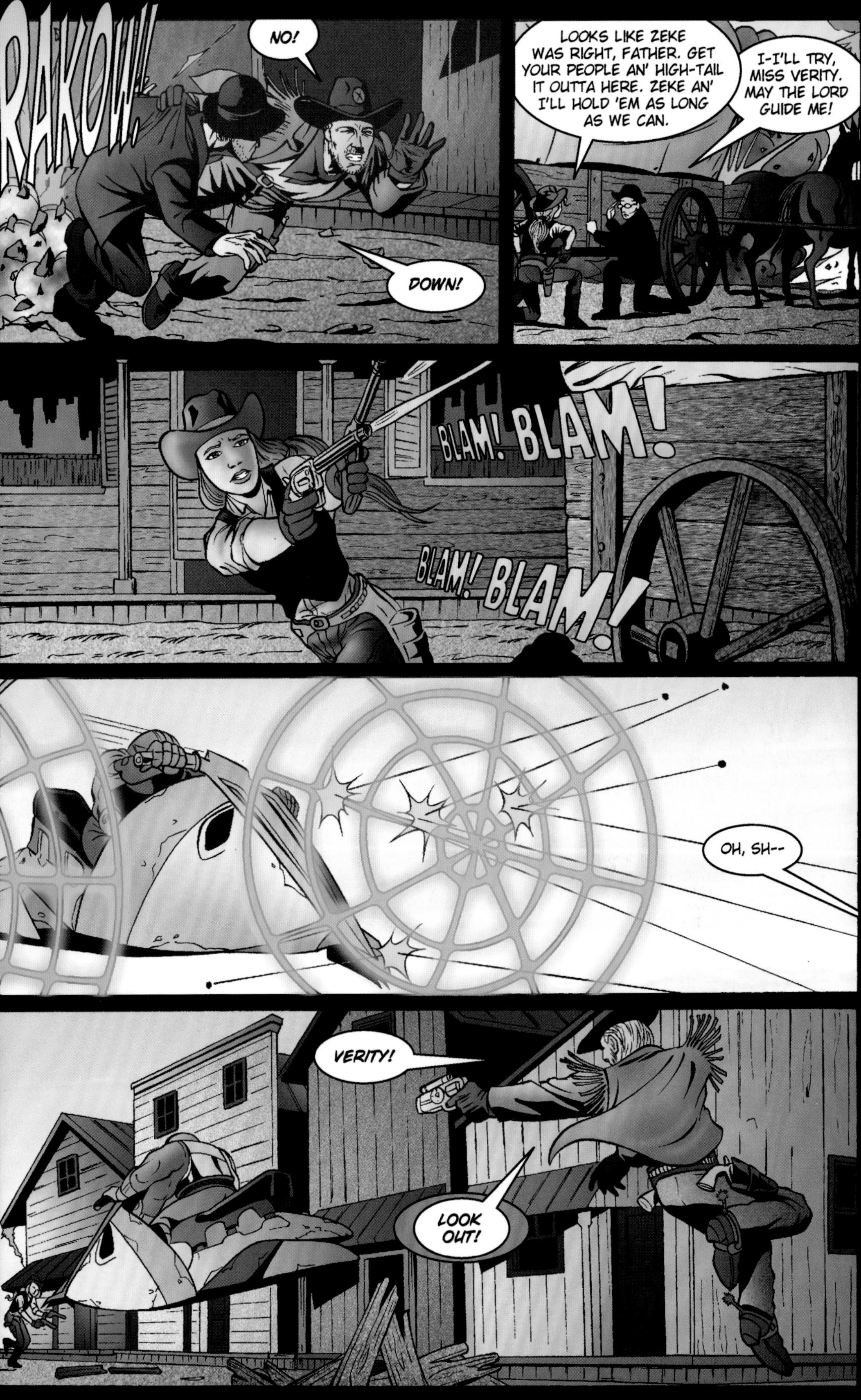
RAKOW!!
NO!
DOWN!
LOOKS LIKE ZEKE WAS RIGHT, FATHER. GET YOUR PEOPLE AN' HIGH-TAIL IT OUTTA HERE. ZEKE AN' I'LL HOLD 'EM AS LONG AS WE CAN.
I-I'LL TRY, MISS VERITY. MAY THE LORD GUIDE ME!
BLAM! BLAM!
BLAM! BLAM!
OH, SH--
VERITY!
LOOK OUT!

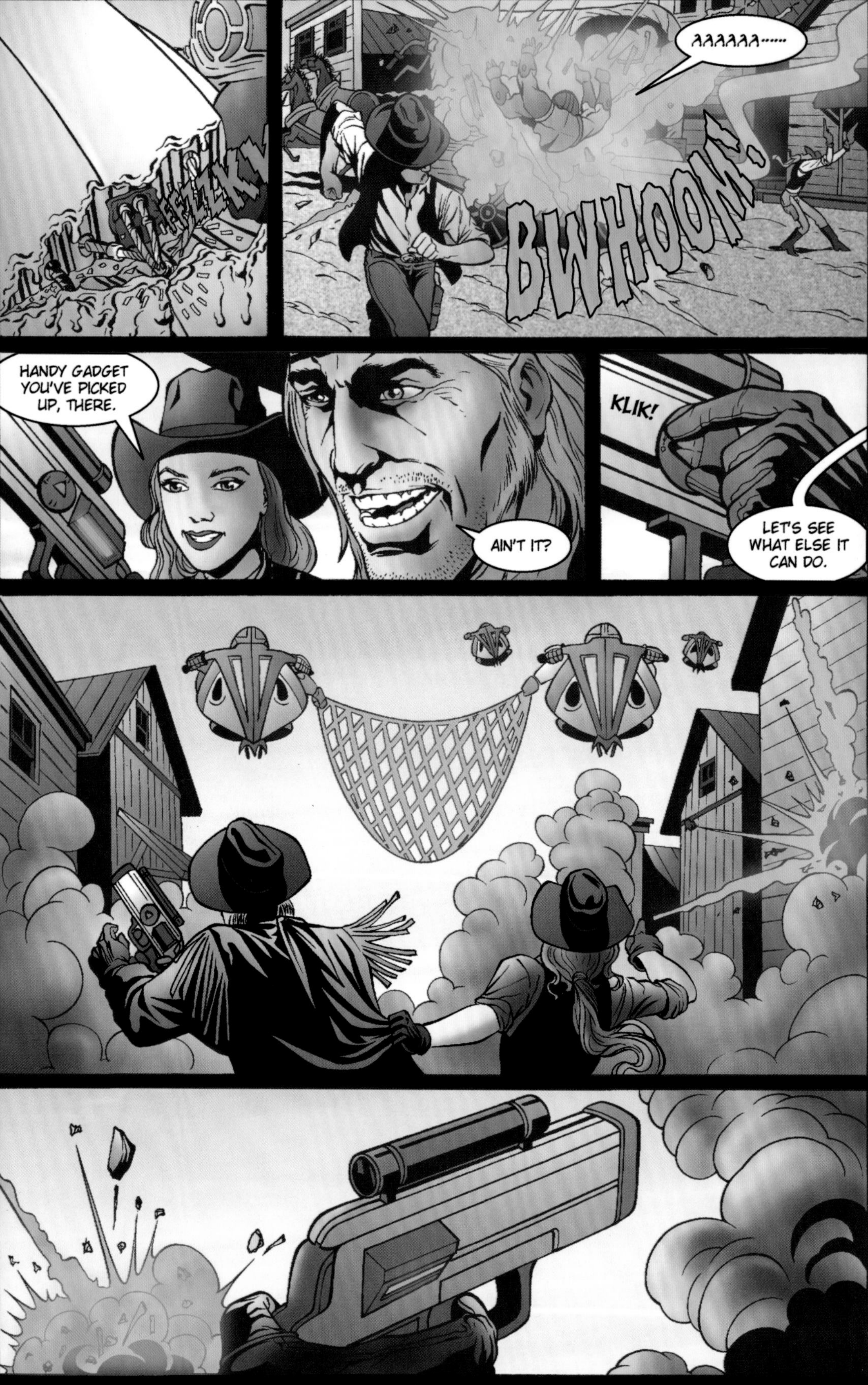
FFZZZK
AAAAAA......
BWHOOM!
HANDY GADGET YOU'VE PICKED UP, THERE.
AIN'T IT?
KLIK!
LET'S SEE WHAT ELSE IT CAN DO.

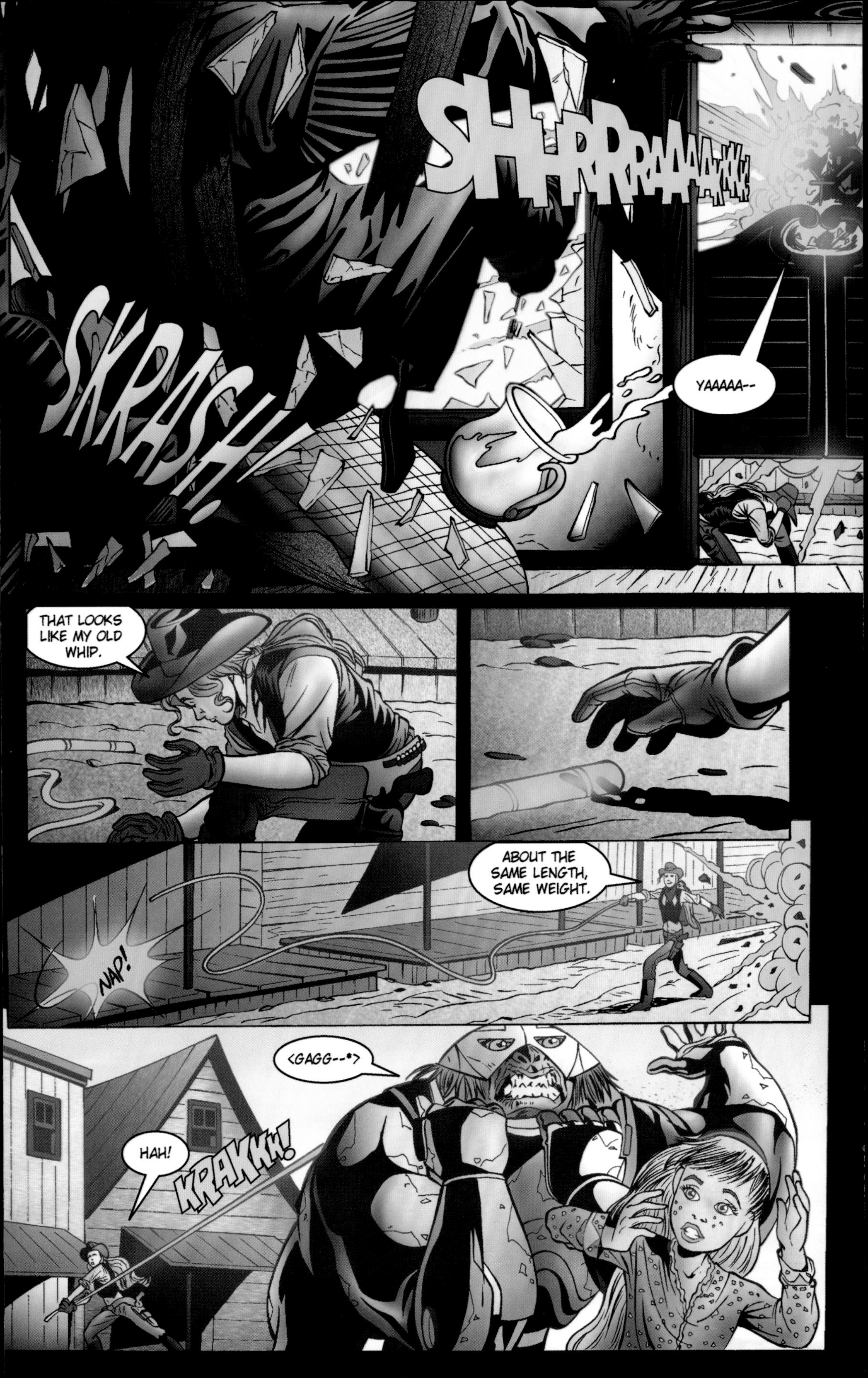
SHRRRAAAAKK!
SKRASH!
YAAAAA--
THAT LOOKS LIKE MY OLD WHIP.
ABOUT THE SAME LENGTH, SAME WEIGHT.
NAP!
<GAGG--*>
HAH!
KRAKKK!

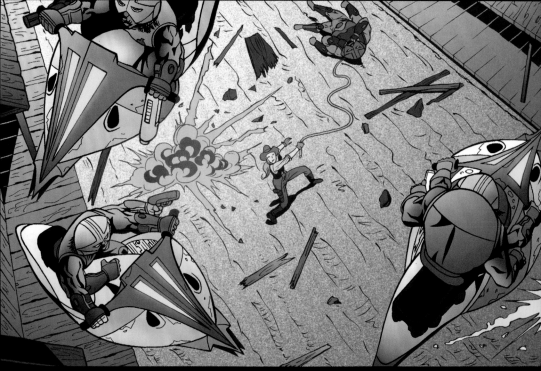

SNAP!

λλλϛ..¯

CRASH!

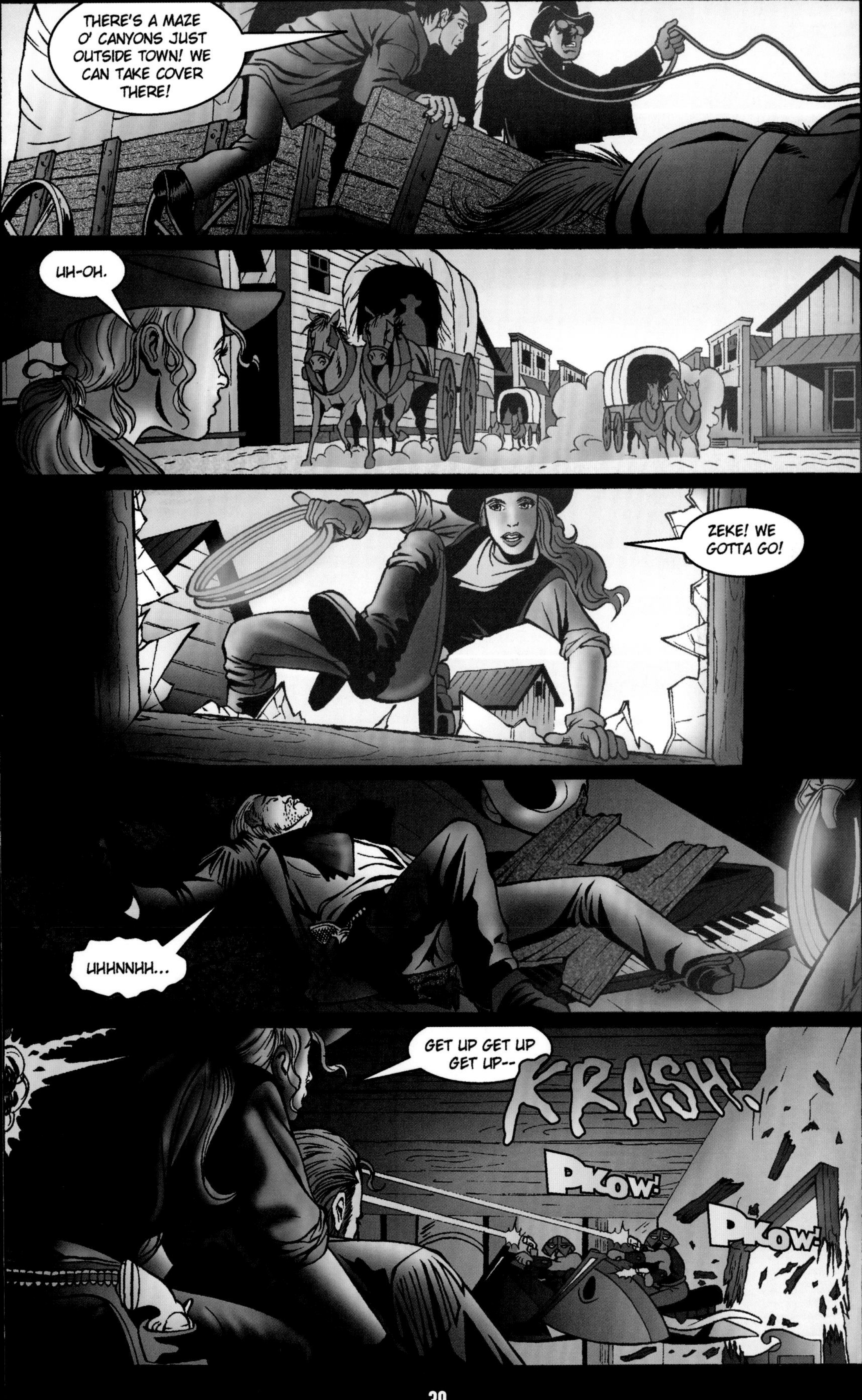
THERE'S A MAZE O' CANYONS JUST OUTSIDE TOWN! WE CAN TAKE COVER THERE!
UH-OH.
ZEKE! WE GOTTA GO!
UHHNNHH...
GET UP GET UP GET UP--
KRASH!
PKOW!
PKOW!

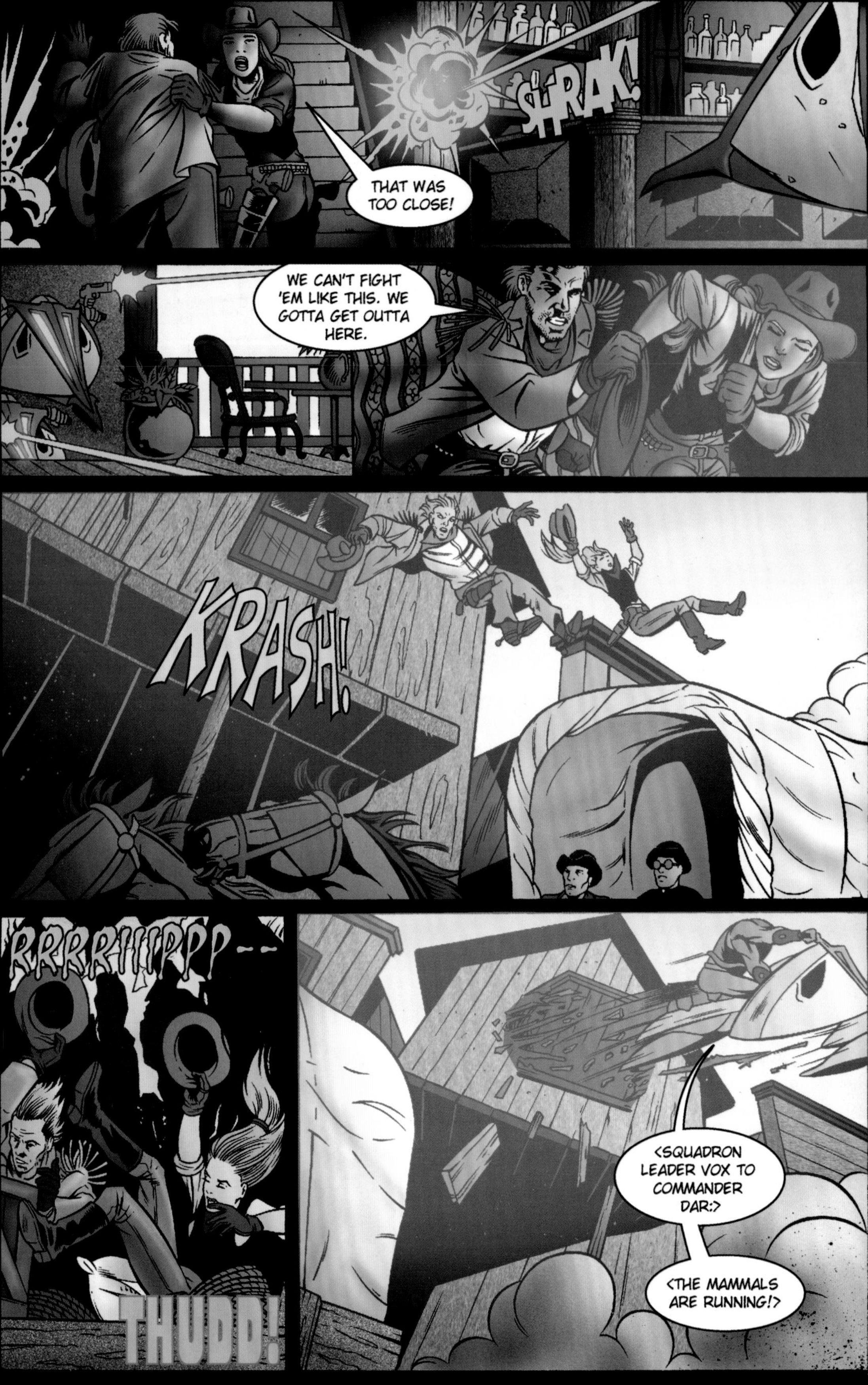
SHRAK!
THAT WAS TOO CLOSE!
WE CAN'T FIGHT 'EM LIKE THIS. WE GOTTA GET OUTTA HERE.
KRASH!
RRRRIIIPPP
THUDD!
<SQUADRON LEADER VOX TO COMMANDER DAR:>
<THE MAMMALS ARE RUNNING!>

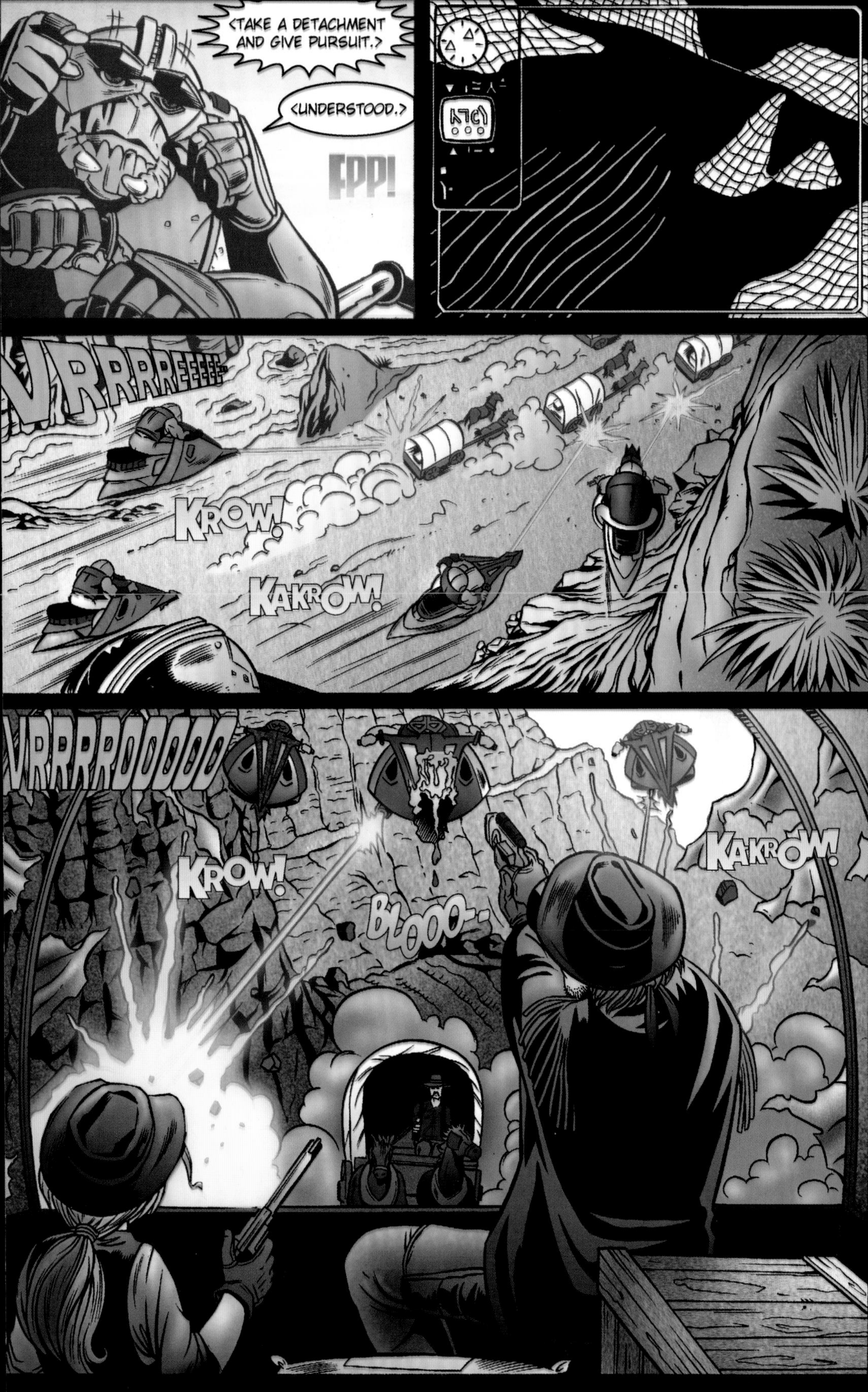
<TAKE A DETACHMENT AND GIVE PURSUIT.>
<UNDERSTOOD.>
FPP!
VRRRRREEEEE
KROW!
KA-KROW!
VRRRROOOOOO
KROW!
BLOOO-
KA-KROW!

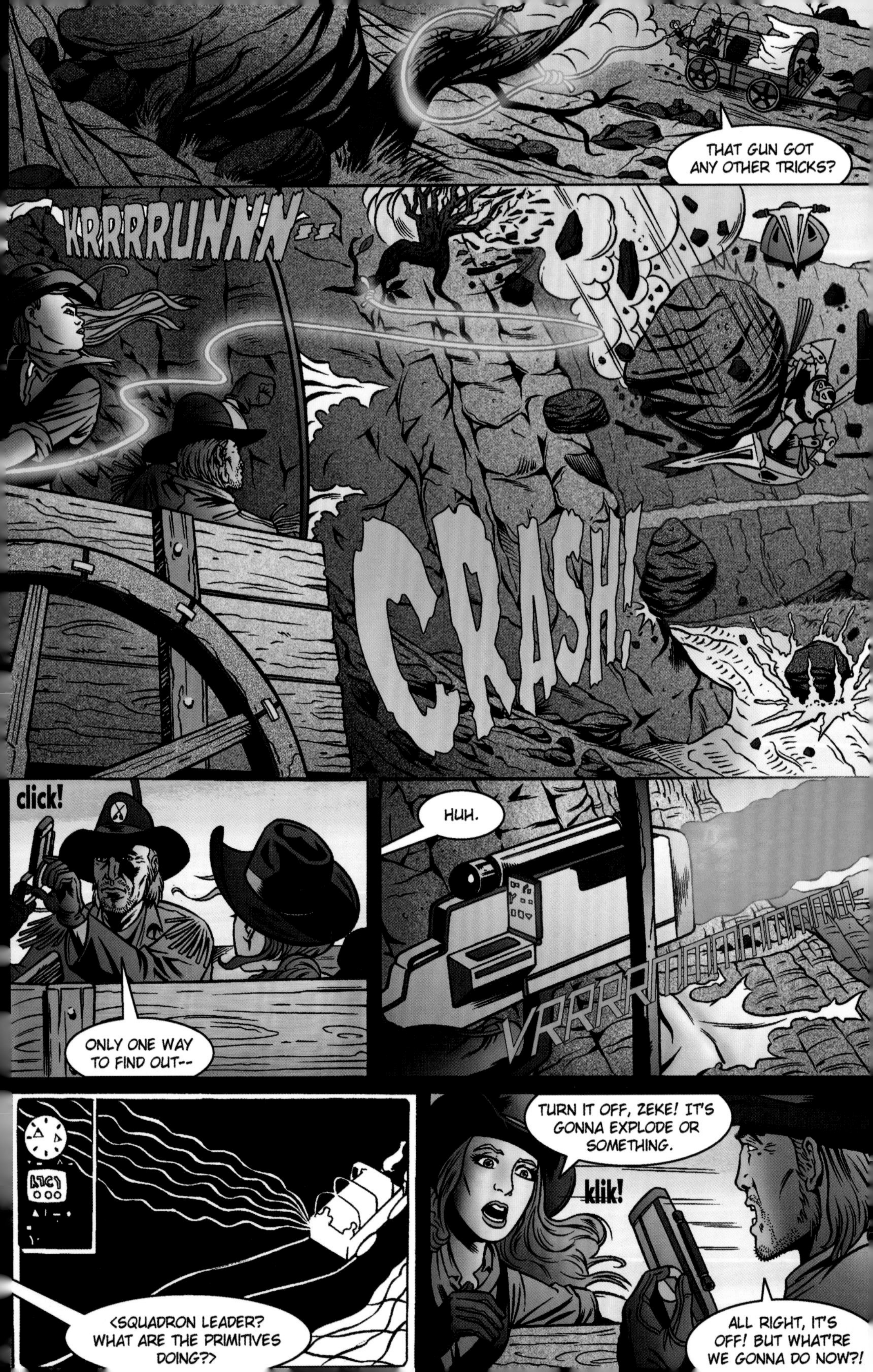

THAT GUN GOT ANY OTHER TRICKS?
KRRRRUNNN--
CRASH!
click!
ONLY ONE WAY TO FIND OUT--
HUH.
VRRRR
<SQUADRON LEADER? WHAT ARE THE PRIMITIVES DOING?>
TURN IT OFF, ZEKE! IT'S GONNA EXPLODE OR SOMETHING.
klik!
ALL RIGHT, IT'S OFF! BUT WHAT'RE WE GONNA DO NOW?!

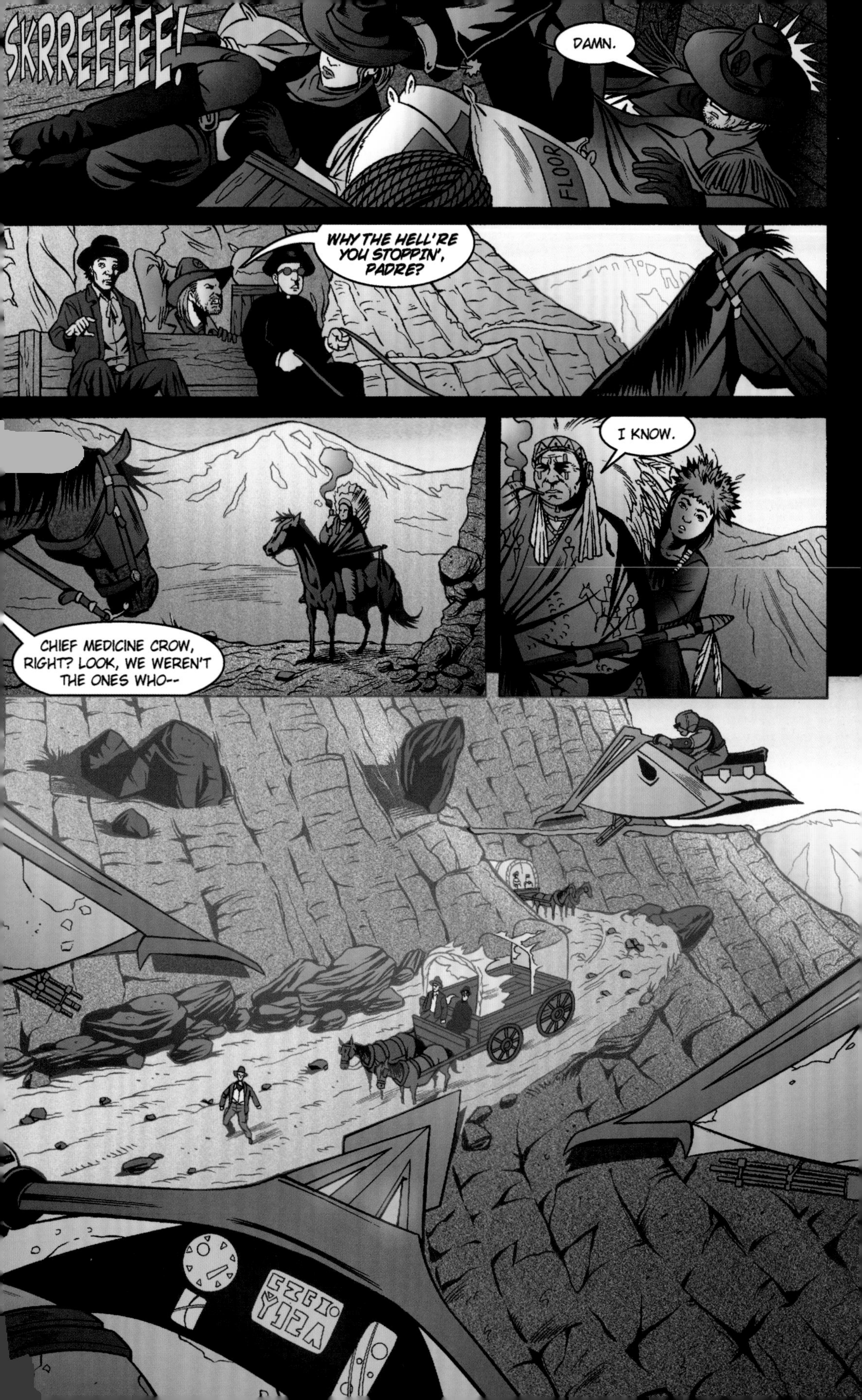
SKRREEEEEE!
DAMN.
FLOOR
WHY THE HELL'RE YOU STOPPIN', PADRE?
CHIEF MEDICINE CROW, RIGHT? LOOK, WE WEREN'T THE ONES WHO--
I KNOW.

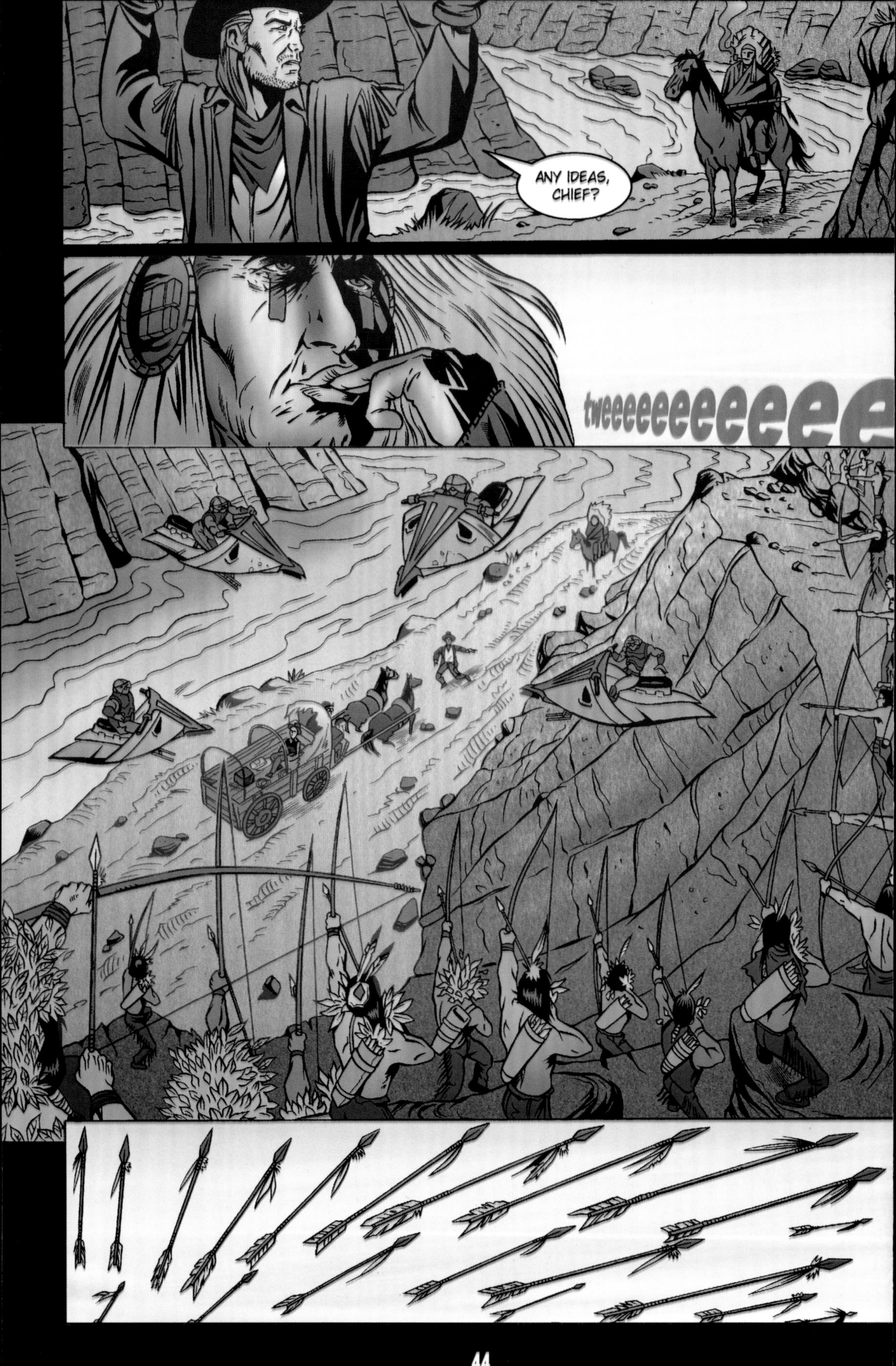

ANY IDEAS, CHIEF?
tweeeeeeeeeee

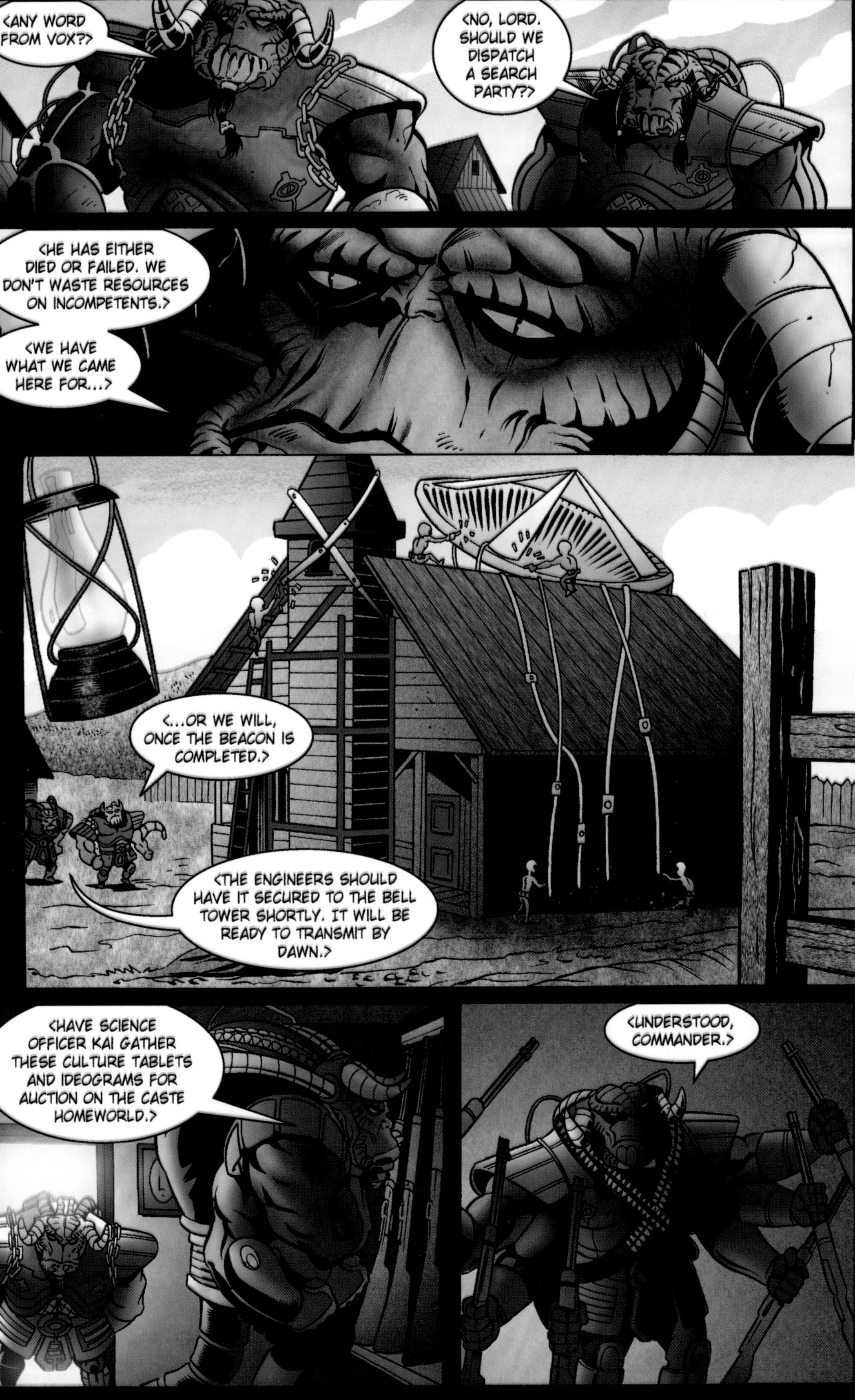
<ANY WORD FROM VOX?>
<NO, LORD. SHOULD WE DISPATCH A SEARCH PARTY?>
<HE HAS EITHER DIED OR FAILED. WE DON'T WASTE RESOURCES ON INCOMPETENTS.>
<WE HAVE WHAT WE CAME HERE FOR...>
<...OR WE WILL, ONCE THE BEACON IS COMPLETED.>
<THE ENGINEERS SHOULD HAVE IT SECURED TO THE BELL TOWER SHORTLY. IT WILL BE READY TO TRANSMIT BY DAWN.>
<HAVE SCIENCE OFFICER KAI GATHER THESE CULTURE TABLETS AND IDEOGRAMS FOR AUCTION ON THE CASTE HOMEWORLD.>
<UNDERSTOOD, COMMANDER.>

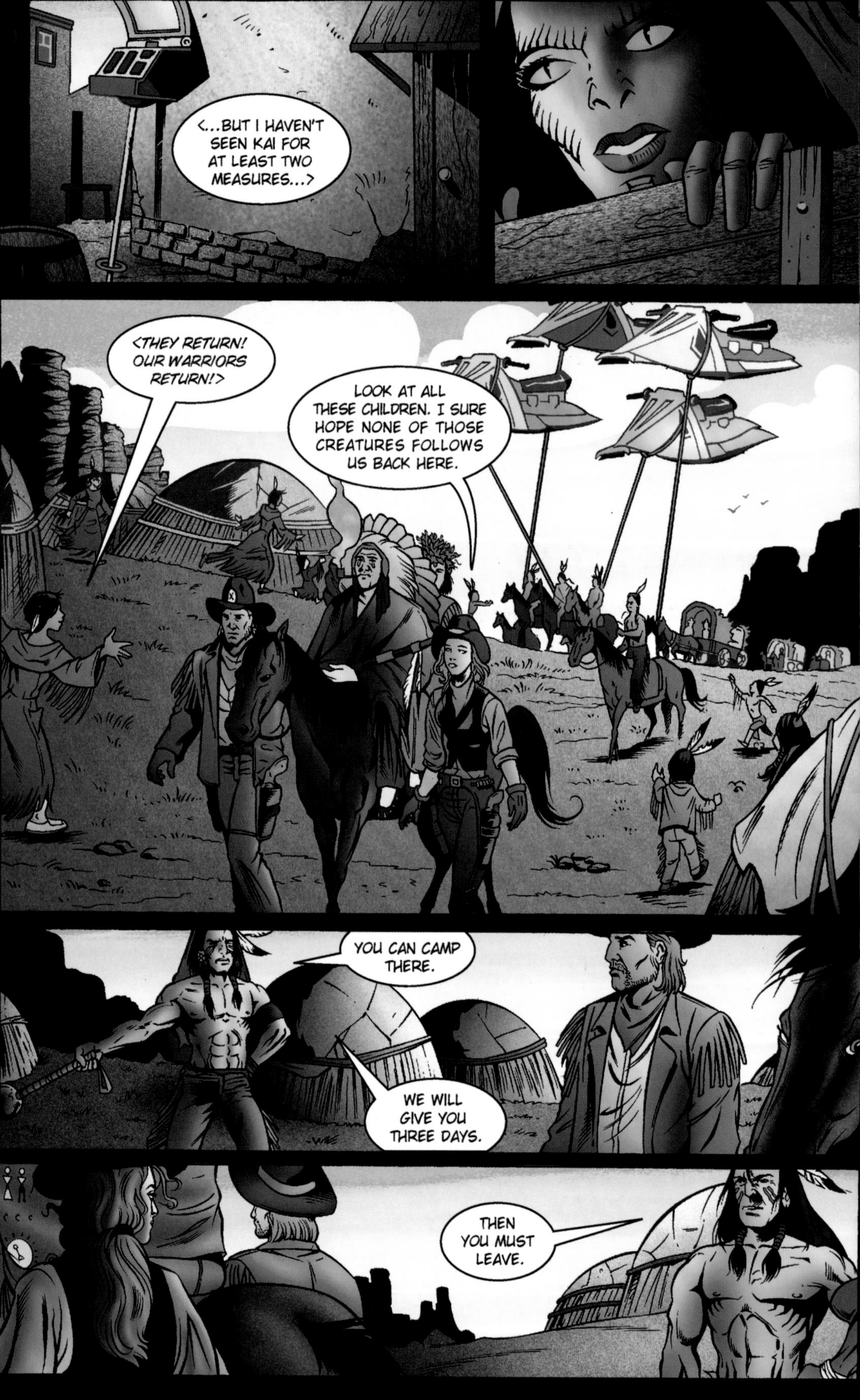
<...BUT I HAVEN'T SEEN KAI FOR AT LEAST TWO MEASURES...>
<THEY RETURN! OUR WARRIORS RETURN!>
LOOK AT ALL THESE CHILDREN. I SURE HOPE NONE OF THOSE CREATURES FOLLOWS US BACK HERE.
YOU CAN CAMP THERE.
WE WILL GIVE YOU THREE DAYS.
THEN YOU MUST LEAVE.

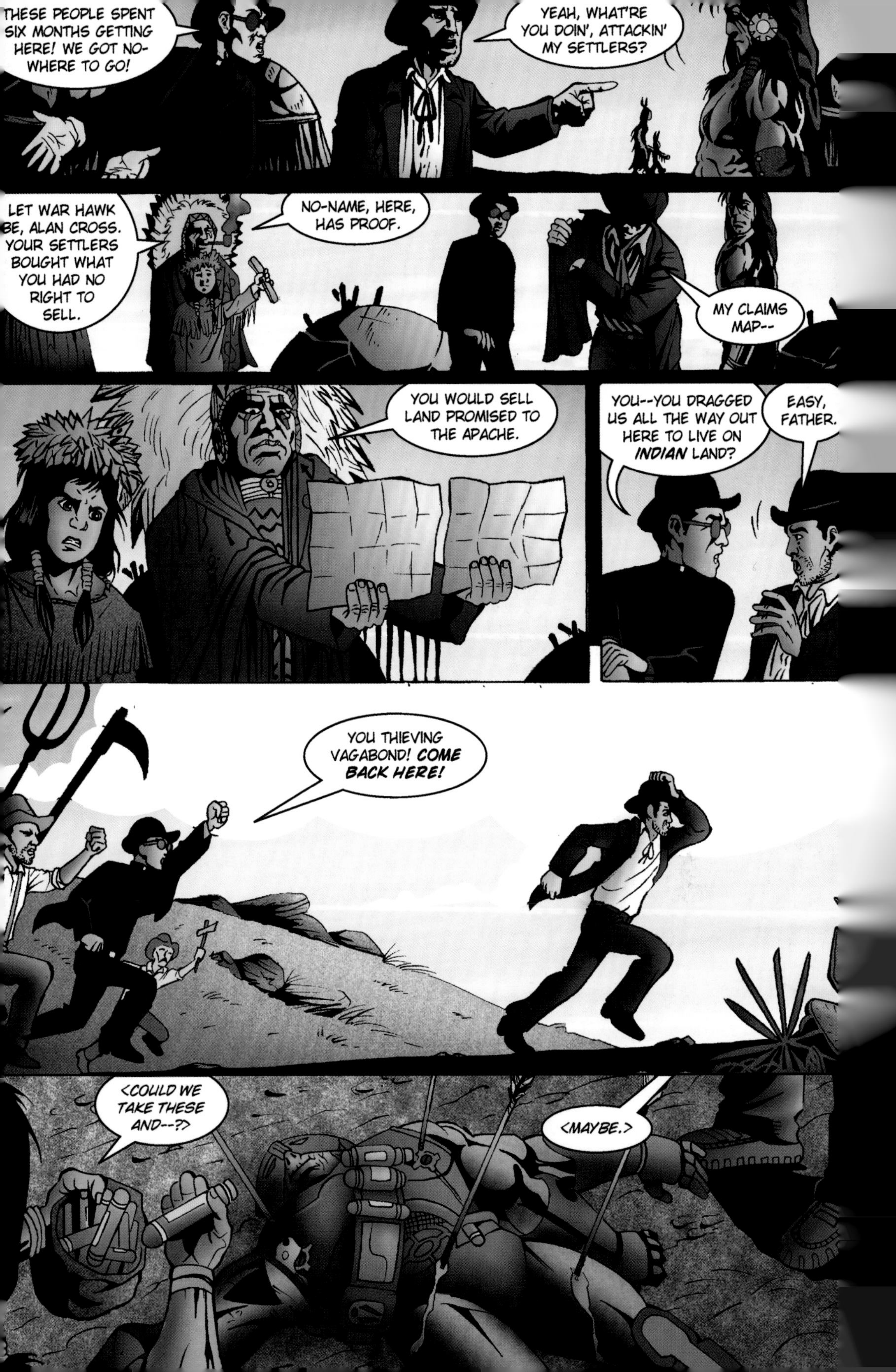

THESE PEOPLE SPENT SIX MONTHS GETTING HERE! WE GOT NO-WHERE TO GO!
YEAH, WHAT'RE YOU DOIN', ATTACKIN' MY SETTLERS?
LET WAR HAWK BE, ALAN CROSS. YOUR SETTLERS BOUGHT WHAT YOU HAD NO RIGHT TO SELL.
NO-NAME, HERE, HAS PROOF.
MY CLAIMS MAP--
YOU WOULD SELL LAND PROMISED TO THE APACHE.
YOU--YOU DRAGGED US ALL THE WAY OUT HERE TO LIVE ON INDIAN LAND?
EASY, FATHER.
YOU THIEVING VAGABOND! COME BACK HERE!
<COULD WE TAKE THESE AND--?>
<MAYBE.>

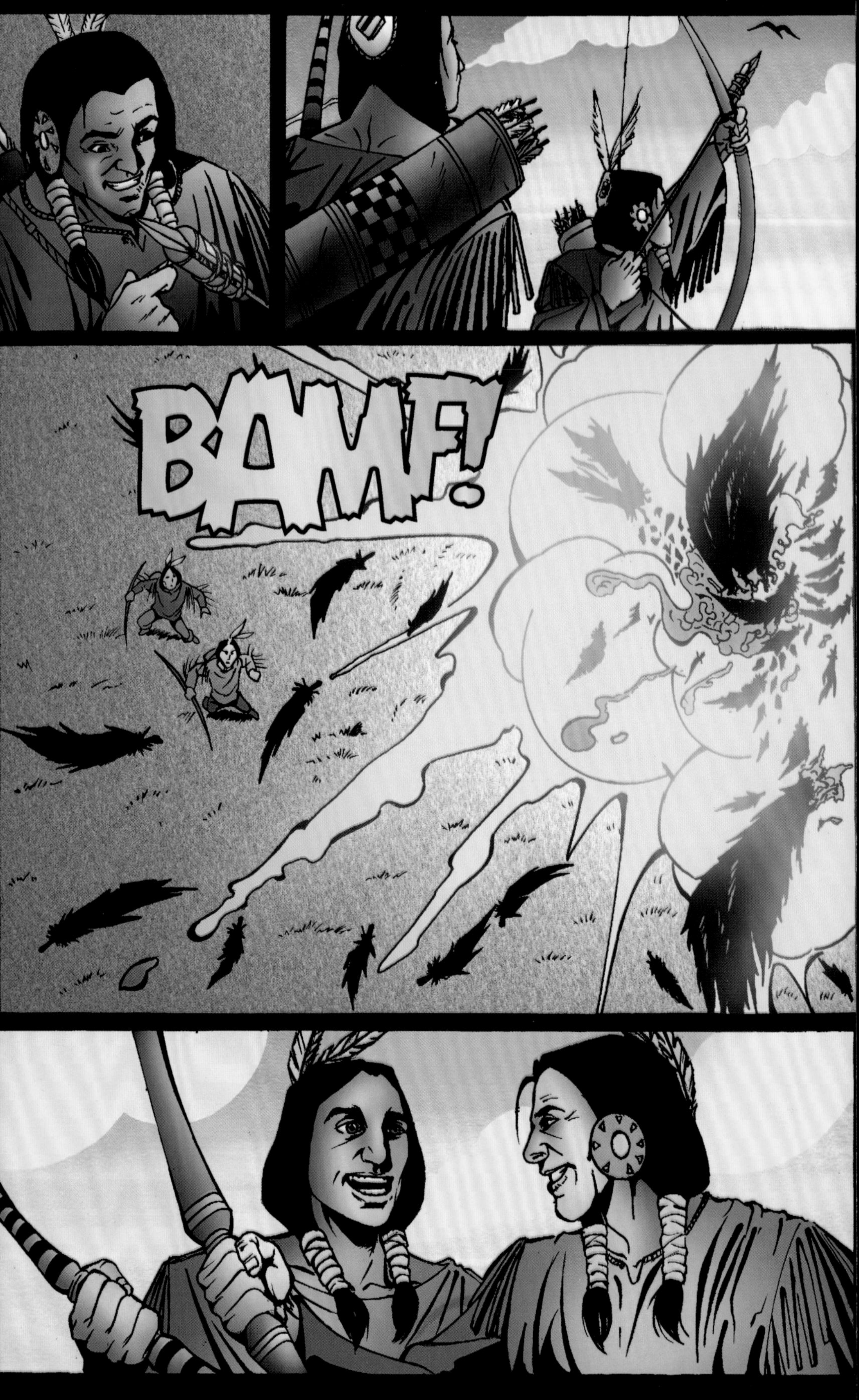
BAMF!

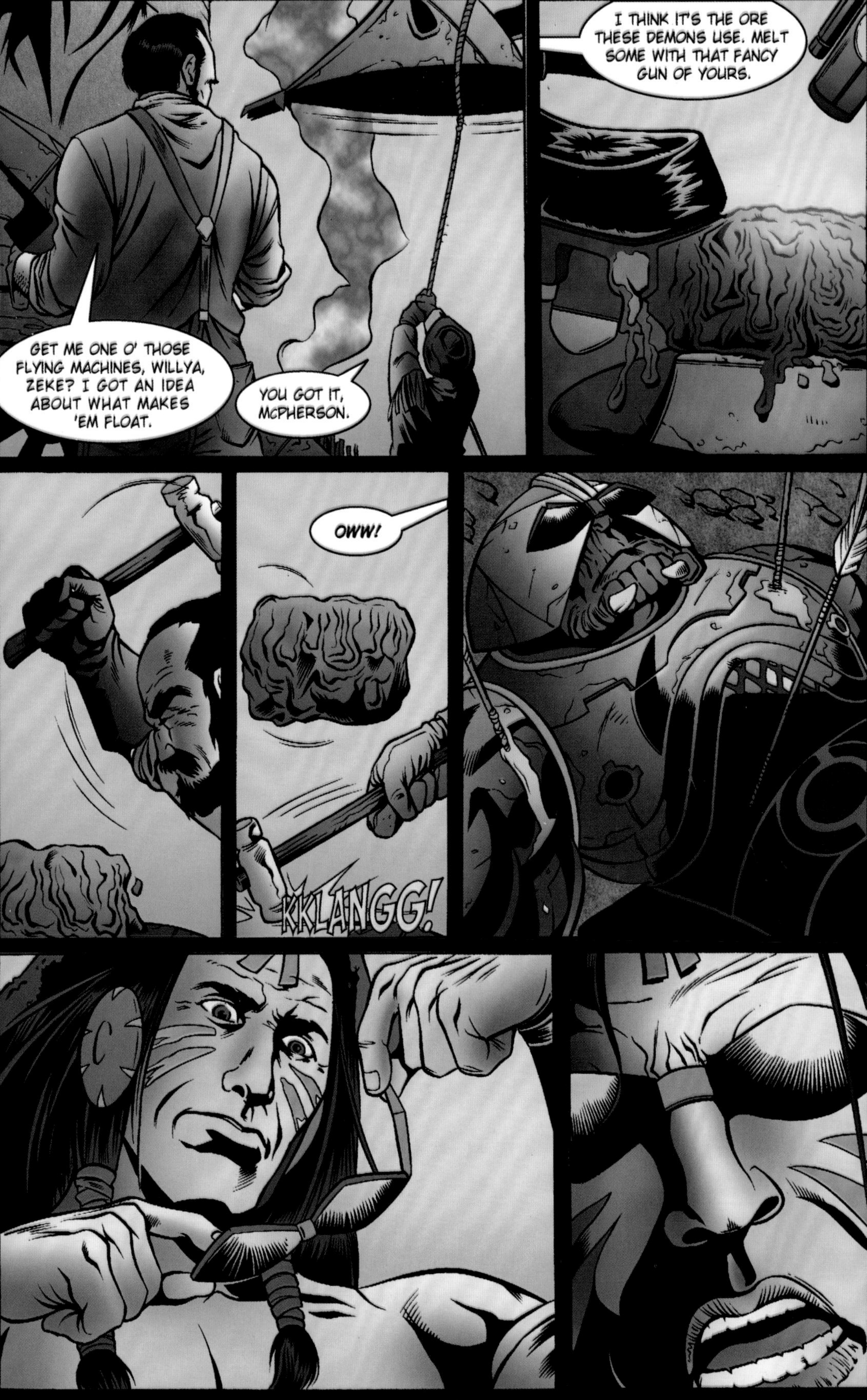
GET ME ONE O' THOSE FLYING MACHINES, WILLYA, ZEKE? I GOT AN IDEA ABOUT WHAT MAKES 'EM FLOAT.
YOU GOT IT, McPHERSON.
I THINK IT'S THE ORE THESE DEMONS USE. MELT SOME WITH THAT FANCY GUN OF YOURS.
OWW!
KKLANGG!

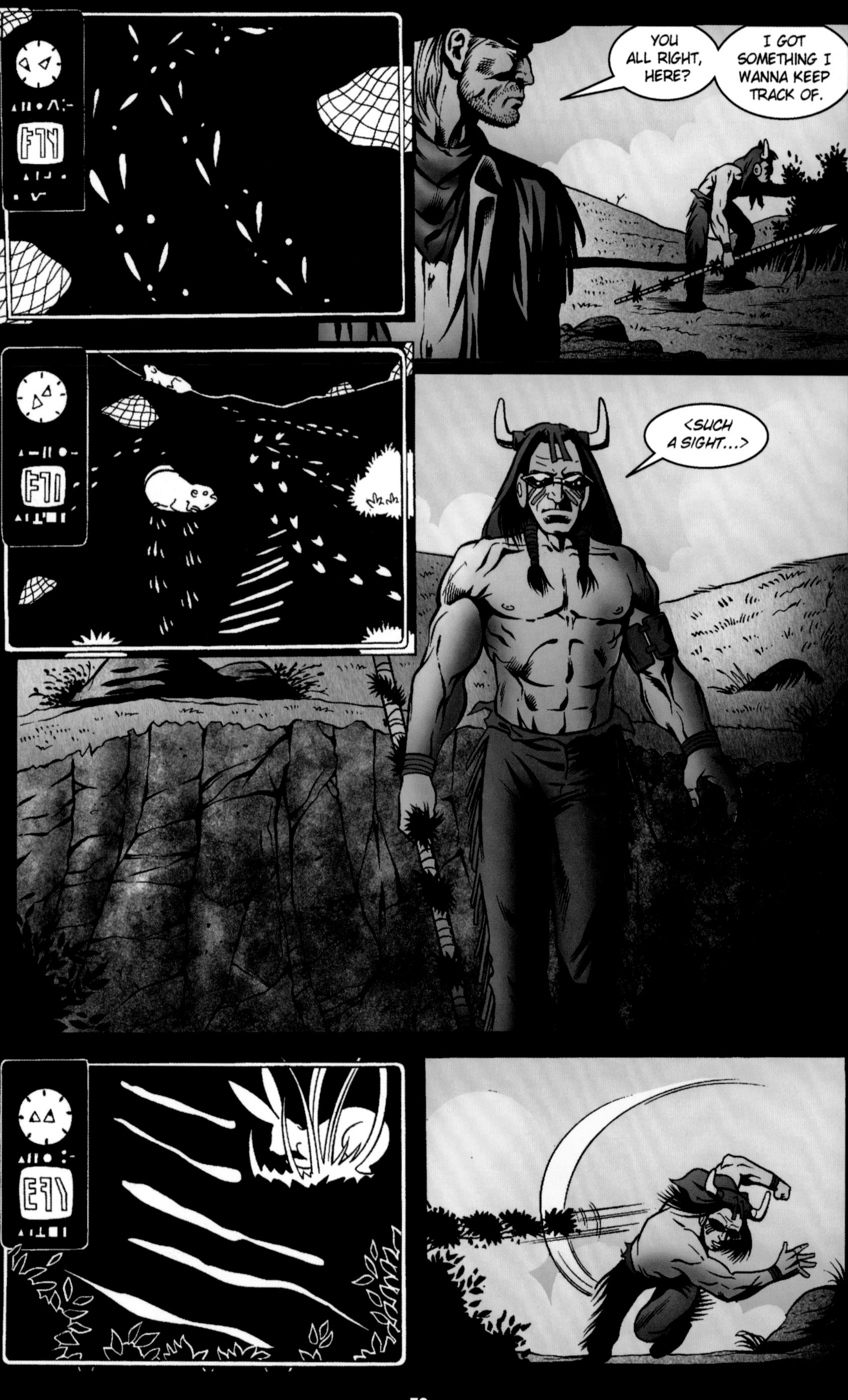
YOU ALL RIGHT, HERE?
I GOT SOMETHING I WANNA KEEP TRACK OF.
<SUCH A SIGHT...>

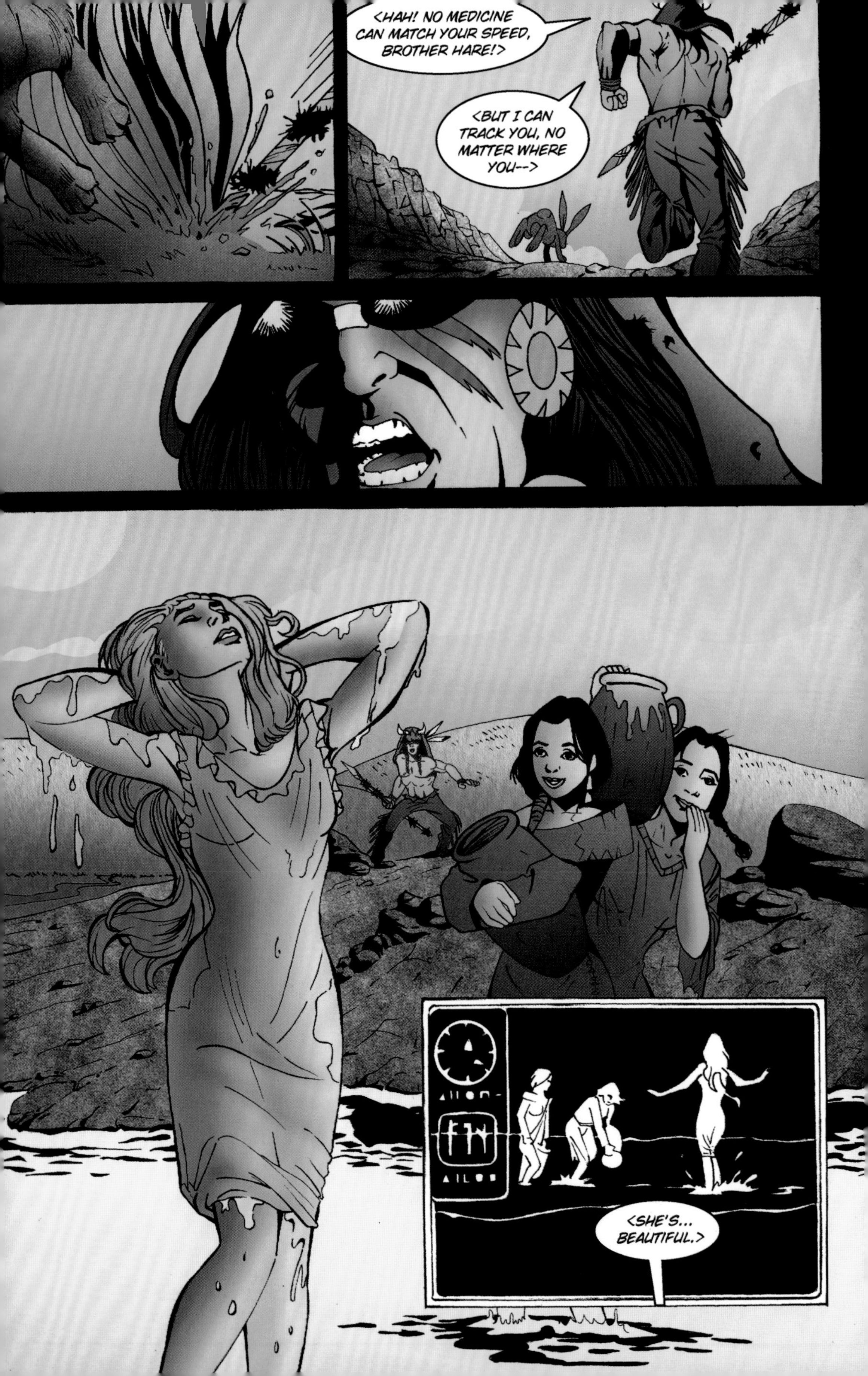
<HAH! NO MEDICINE CAN MATCH YOUR SPEED, BROTHER HARE!>
<BUT I CAN TRACK YOU, NO MATTER WHERE YOU-->
<SHE'S... BEAUTIFUL.>

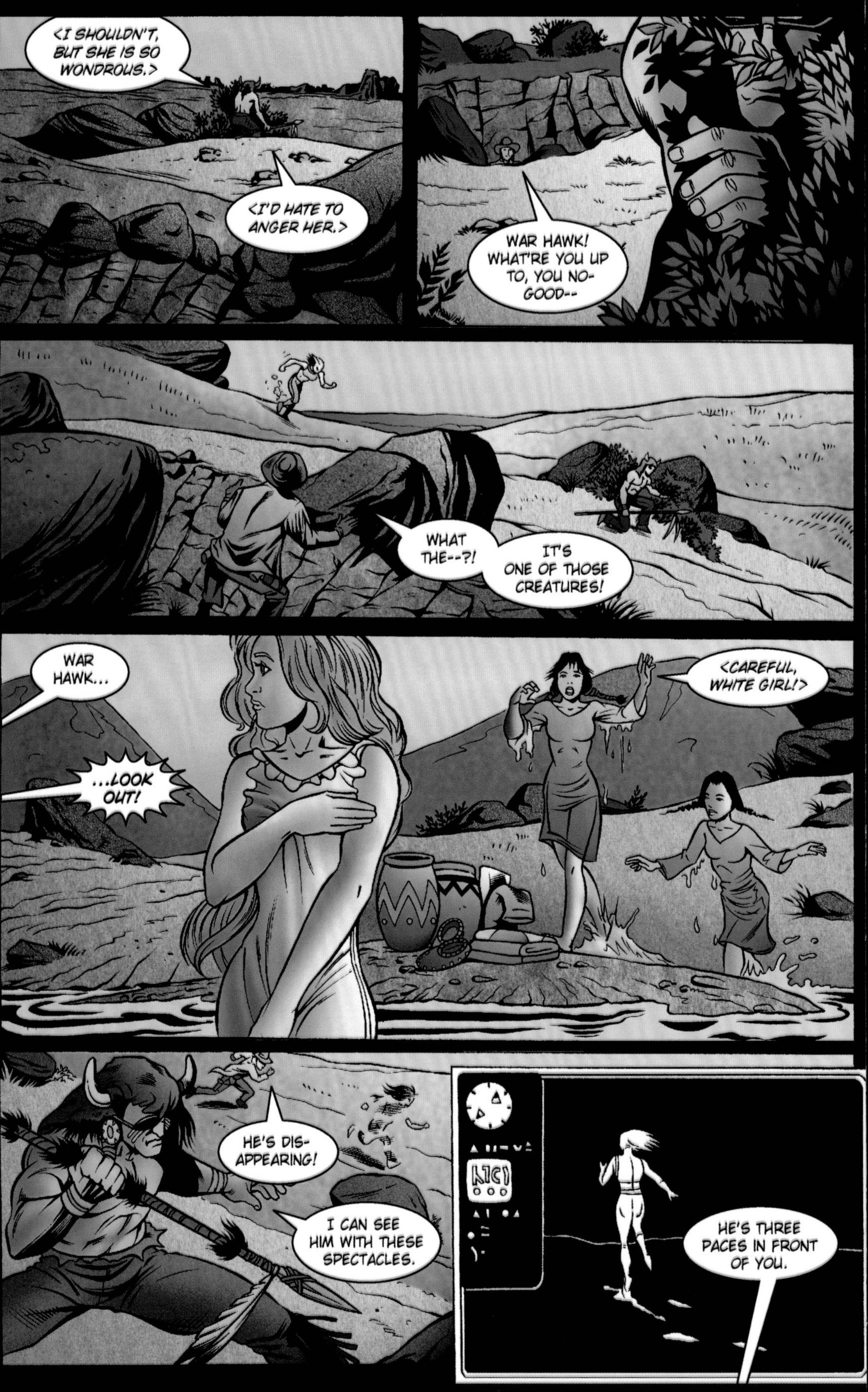
<I SHOULDN'T, BUT SHE IS SO WONDROUS.>
<I'D HATE TO ANGER HER.>
WAR HAWK! WHAT'RE YOU UP TO, YOU NO-GOOD--
WHAT THE--?!
IT'S ONE OF THOSE CREATURES!
WAR HAWK...
...LOOK OUT!
<CAREFUL, WHITE GIRL!>
HE'S DIS-APPEARING!
I CAN SEE HIM WITH THESE SPECTACLES.
HE'S THREE PACES IN FRONT OF YOU.

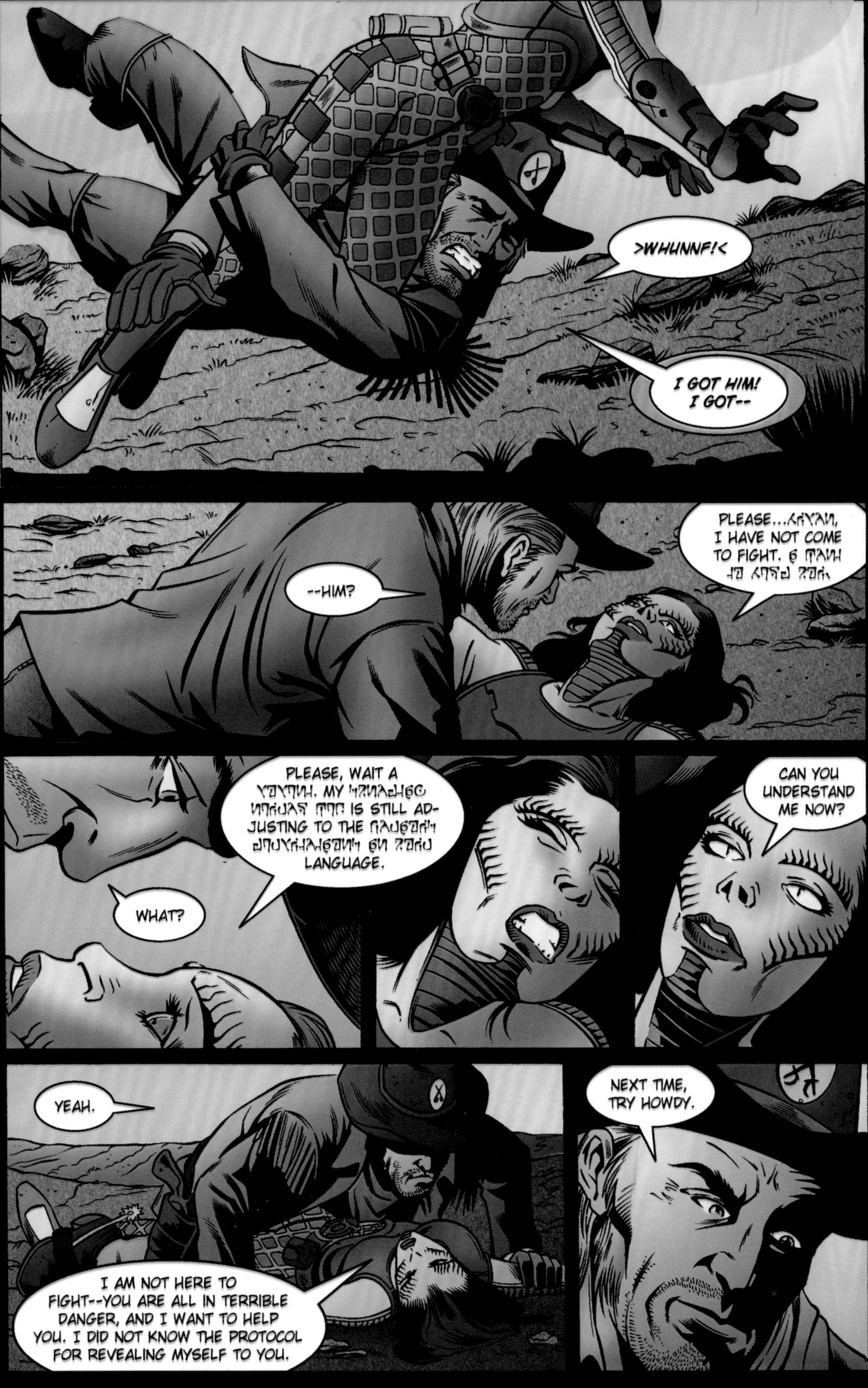
>WHUNNF!<
I GOT HIM! I GOT--
--HIM?
PLEASE... I HAVE NOT COME TO FIGHT.
PLEASE, WAIT A . MY IS STILL AD-JUSTING TO THE LANGUAGE.
WHAT?
CAN YOU UNDERSTAND ME NOW?
YEAH.
I AM NOT HERE TO FIGHT--YOU ARE ALL IN TERRIBLE DANGER, AND I WANT TO HELP YOU. I DID NOT KNOW THE PROTOCOL FOR REVEALING MYSELF TO YOU.
NEXT TIME, TRY HOWDY.

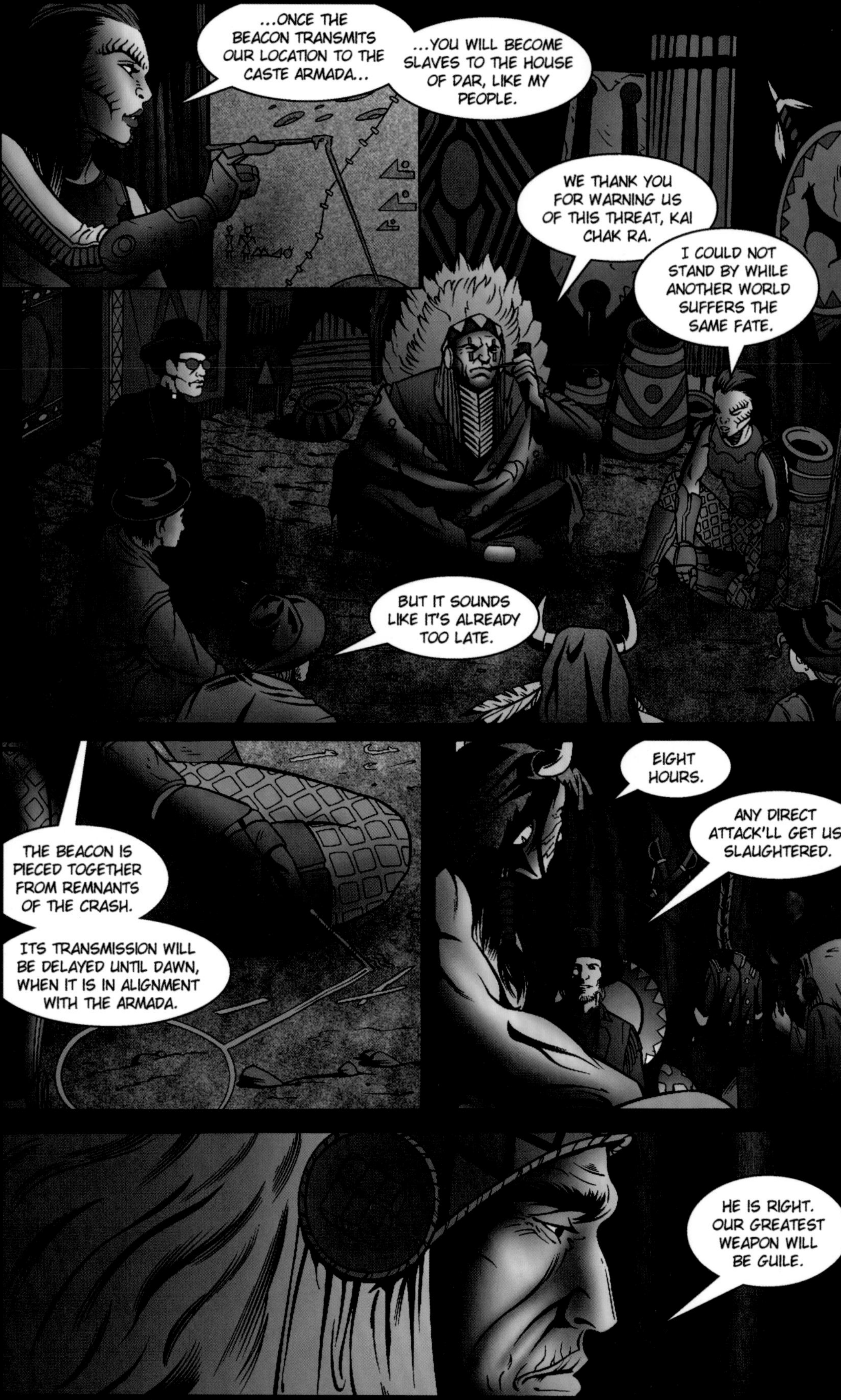
...ONCE THE BEACON TRANSMITS OUR LOCATION TO THE CASTE ARMADA...
...YOU WILL BECOME SLAVES TO THE HOUSE OF DAR, LIKE MY PEOPLE.
WE THANK YOU FOR WARNING US OF THIS THREAT, KAI CHAK RA.
I COULD NOT STAND BY WHILE ANOTHER WORLD SUFFERS THE SAME FATE.
BUT IT SOUNDS LIKE IT'S ALREADY TOO LATE.
THE BEACON IS PIECED TOGETHER FROM REMNANTS OF THE CRASH.
ITS TRANSMISSION WILL BE DELAYED UNTIL DAWN, WHEN IT IS IN ALIGNMENT WITH THE ARMADA.
EIGHT HOURS.
ANY DIRECT ATTACK'LL GET US SLAUGHTERED.
HE IS RIGHT. OUR GREATEST WEAPON WILL BE GUILE.

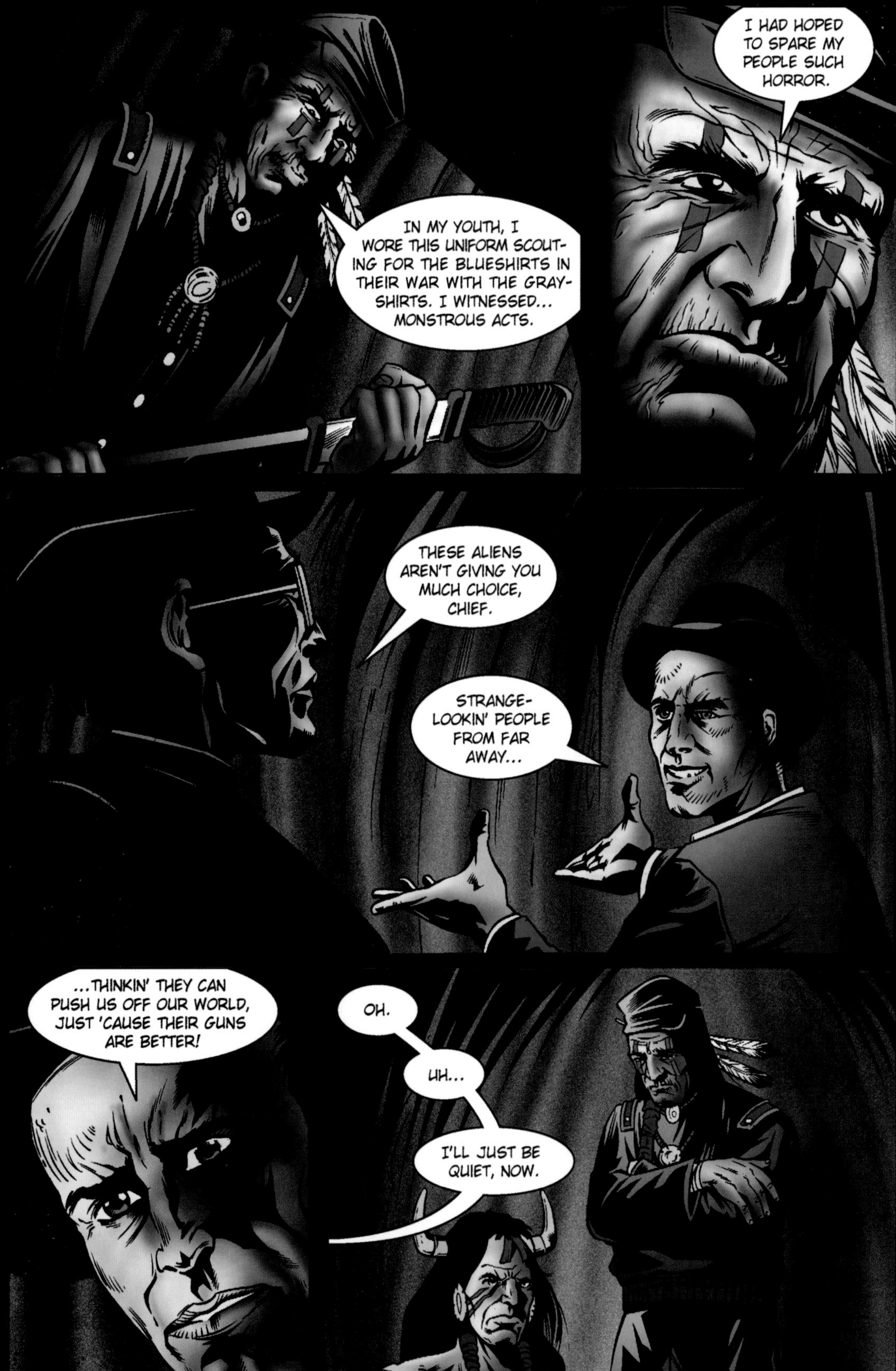
IN MY YOUTH, I WORE THIS UNIFORM SCOUTING FOR THE BLUESHIRTS IN THEIR WAR WITH THE GRAYSHIRTS. I WITNESSED... MONSTROUS ACTS.
I HAD HOPED TO SPARE MY PEOPLE SUCH HORROR.
THESE ALIENS AREN'T GIVING YOU MUCH CHOICE, CHIEF.
STRANGE-LOOKIN' PEOPLE FROM FAR AWAY...
...THINKIN' THEY CAN PUSH US OFF OUR WORLD, JUST 'CAUSE THEIR GUNS ARE BETTER!
OH.
UH...
I'LL JUST BE QUIET, NOW.

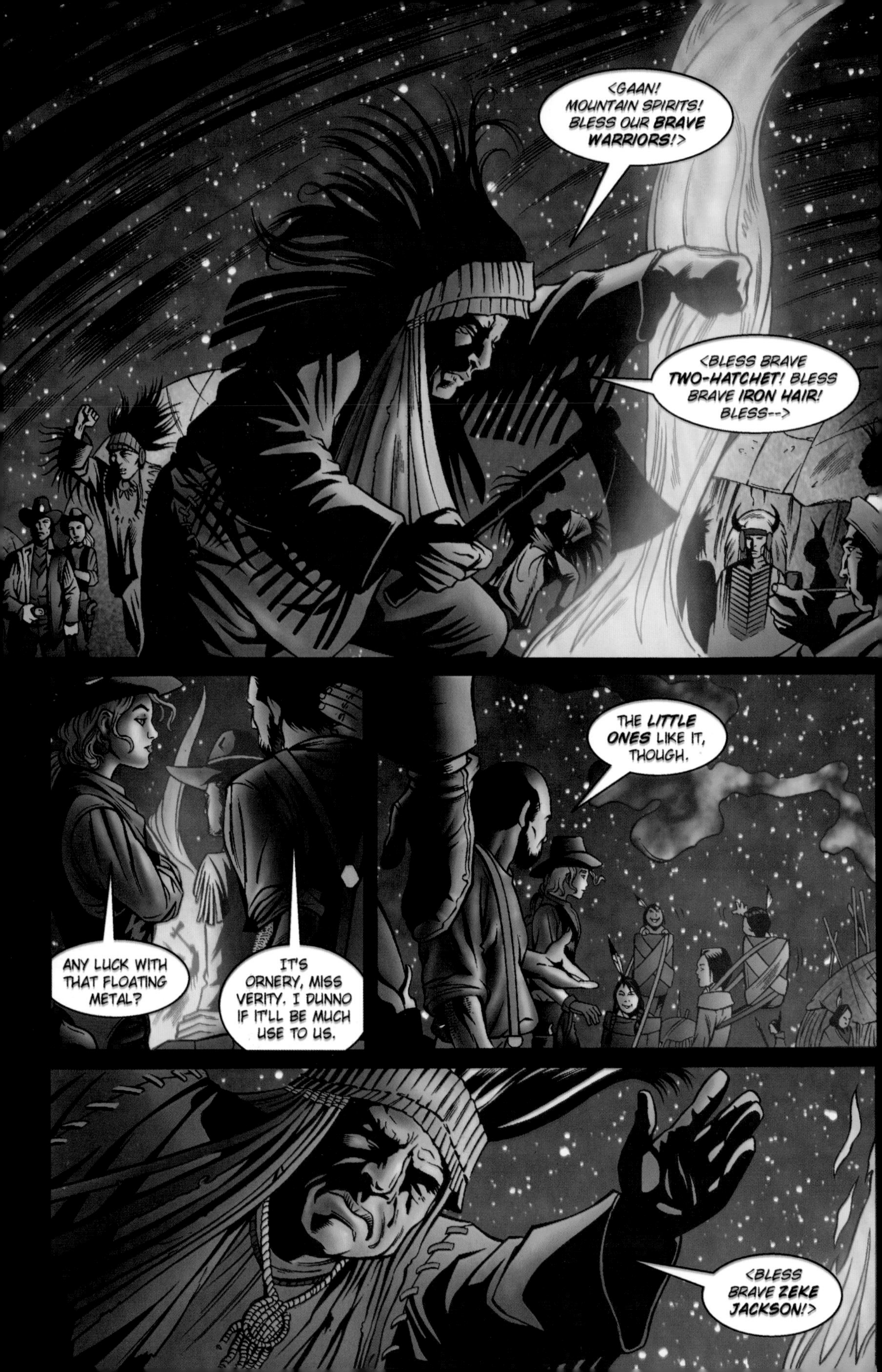
<GAAN! MOUNTAIN SPIRITS! BLESS OUR **BRAVE WARRIORS!**>
<BLESS BRAVE **TWO-HATCHET!** BLESS BRAVE **IRON HAIR!** BLESS-->
ANY LUCK WITH THAT FLOATING METAL?
IT'S ORNERY, MISS VERITY. I DUNNO IF IT'LL BE MUCH USE TO US.
THE ***LITTLE ONES*** LIKE IT, THOUGH.
<BLESS BRAVE **ZEKE JACKSON!**>

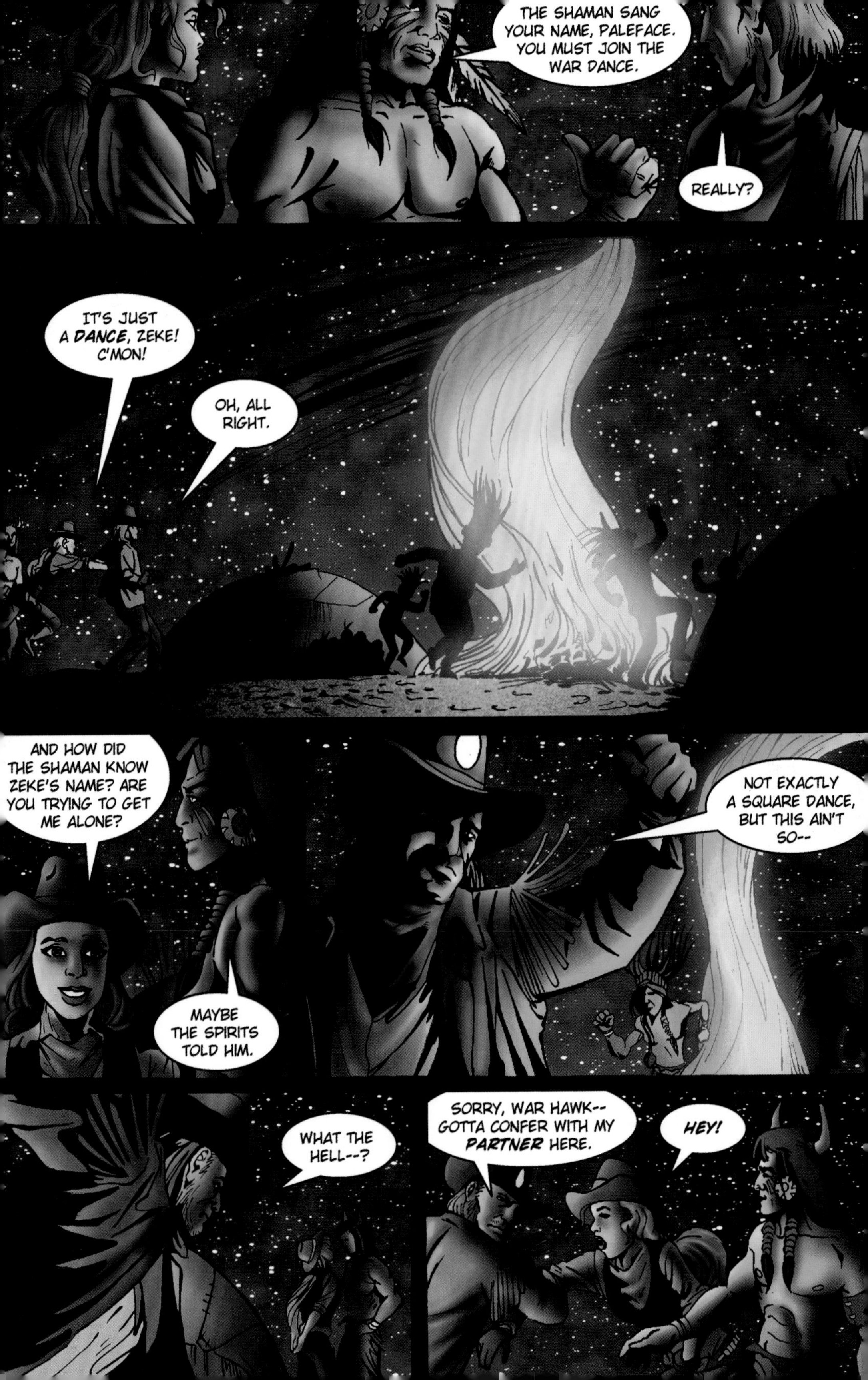
THE SHAMAN SANG YOUR NAME, PALEFACE. YOU MUST JOIN THE WAR DANCE.
REALLY?
IT'S JUST A *DANCE*, ZEKE! C'MON!
OH, ALL RIGHT.
AND HOW DID THE SHAMAN KNOW ZEKE'S NAME? ARE YOU TRYING TO GET ME ALONE?
MAYBE THE SPIRITS TOLD HIM.
NOT EXACTLY A SQUARE DANCE, BUT THIS AIN'T SO--
WHAT THE HELL--?
SORRY, WAR HAWK-- GOTTA CONFER WITH MY *PARTNER* HERE.
HEY!

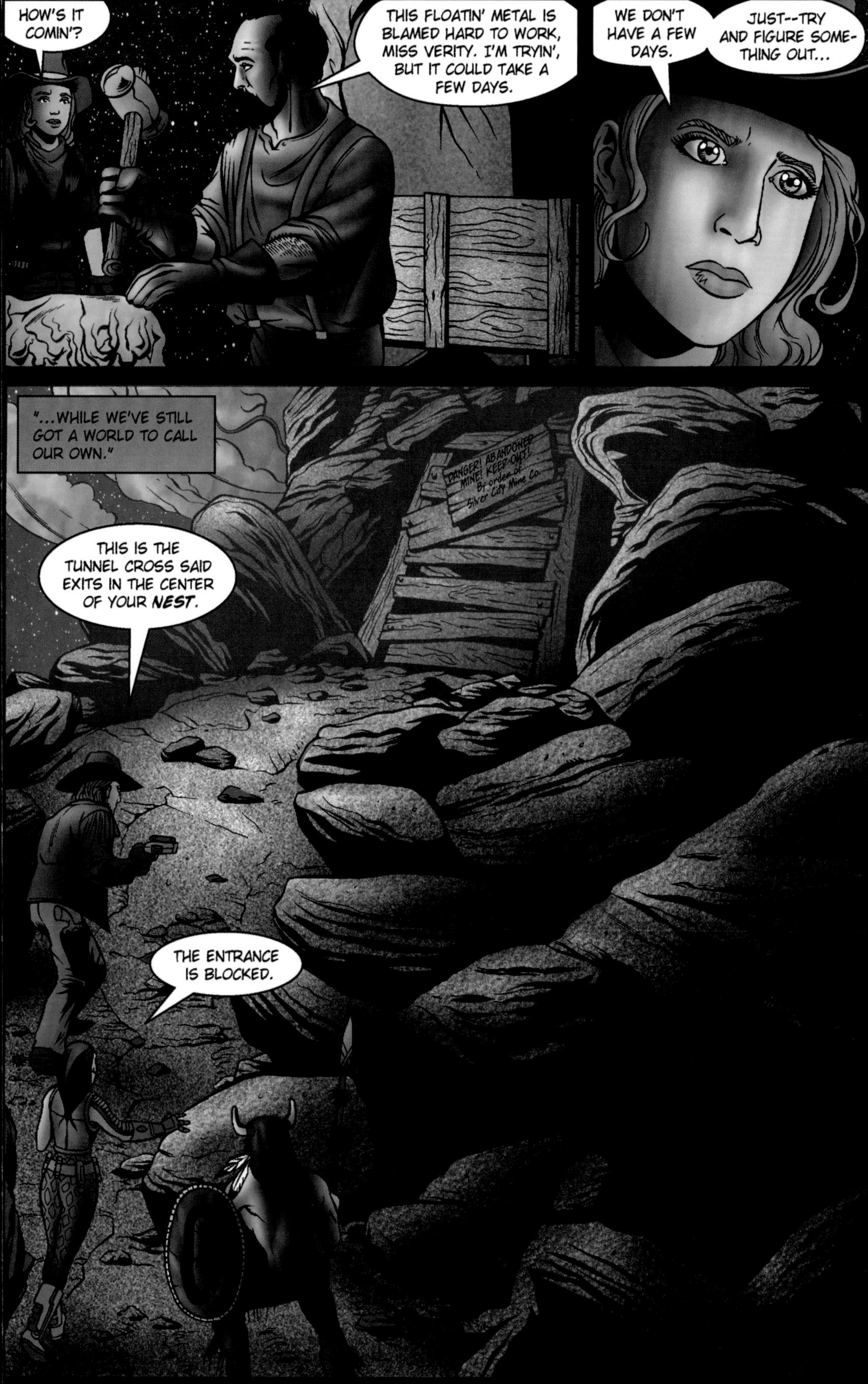
HOW'S IT COMIN'?
THIS FLOATIN' METAL IS BLAMED HARD TO WORK, MISS VERITY. I'M TRYIN', BUT IT COULD TAKE A FEW DAYS.
WE DON'T HAVE A FEW DAYS.
JUST--TRY AND FIGURE SOMETHING OUT...
"...WHILE WE'VE STILL GOT A WORLD TO CALL OUR OWN."
DANGER! ABANDONED MINE! KEEP OUT! By order of Silver City Mine Co.
THIS IS THE TUNNEL CROSS SAID EXITS IN THE CENTER OF YOUR ***NEST***.
THE ENTRANCE IS BLOCKED.

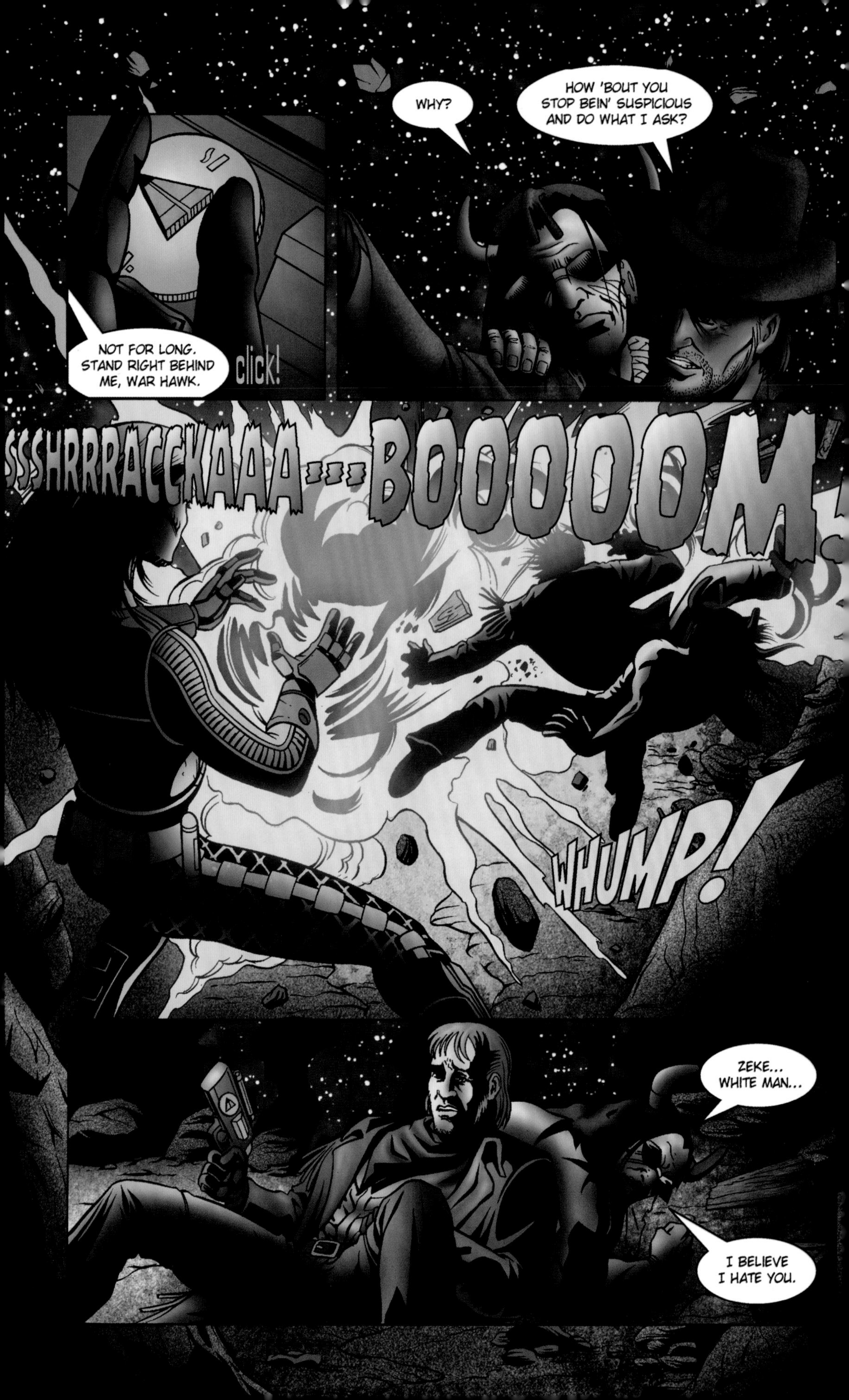
NOT FOR LONG. STAND RIGHT BEHIND ME, WAR HAWK.
click!
WHY?
HOW 'BOUT YOU STOP BEIN' SUSPICIOUS AND DO WHAT I ASK?
SSSHRRRACCKAAA---BOOOOOM!
WHUMP!
ZEKE... WHITE MAN...
I BELIEVE I HATE YOU.

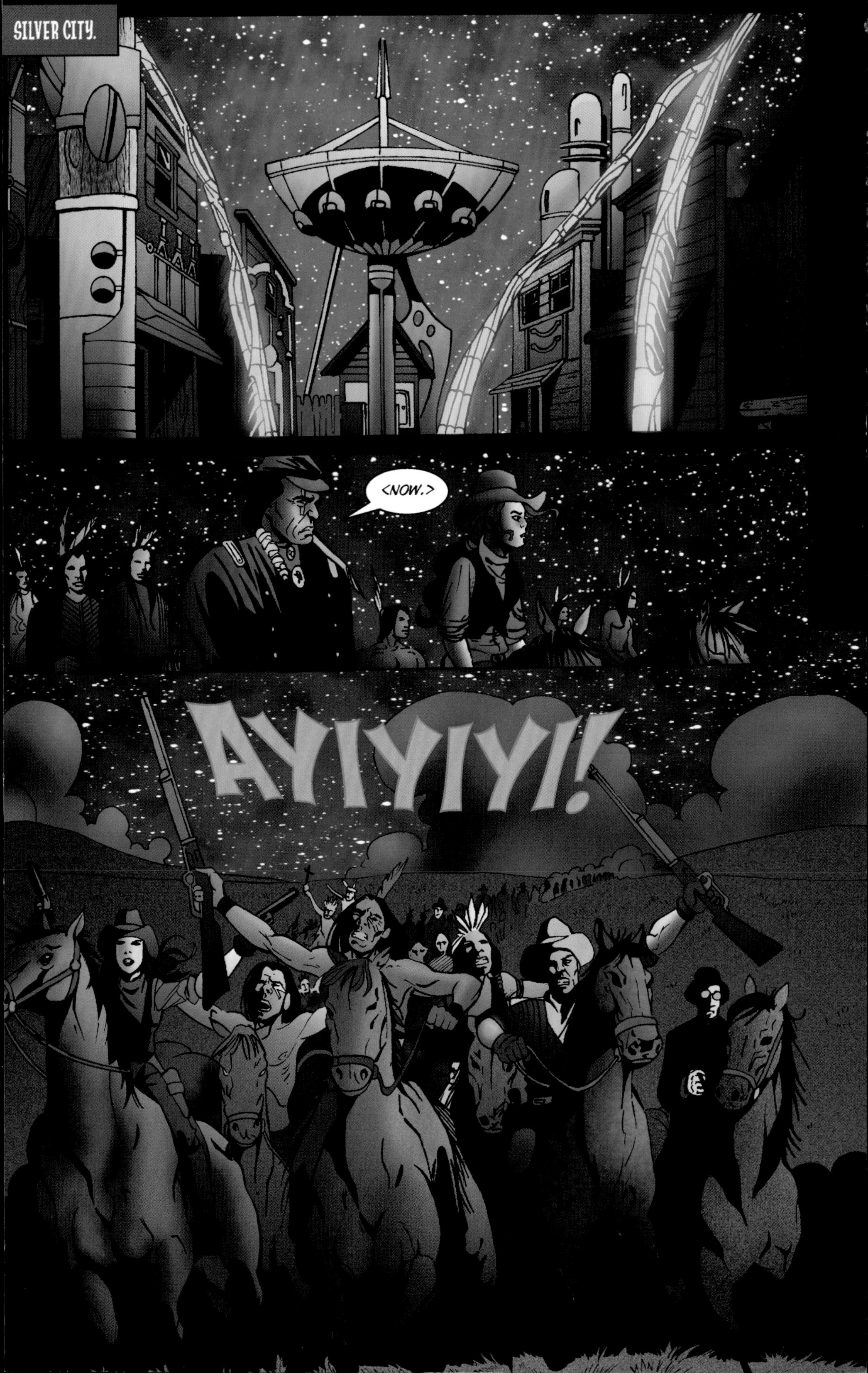
SILVER CITY.
<NOW.>
AYIYIYI!

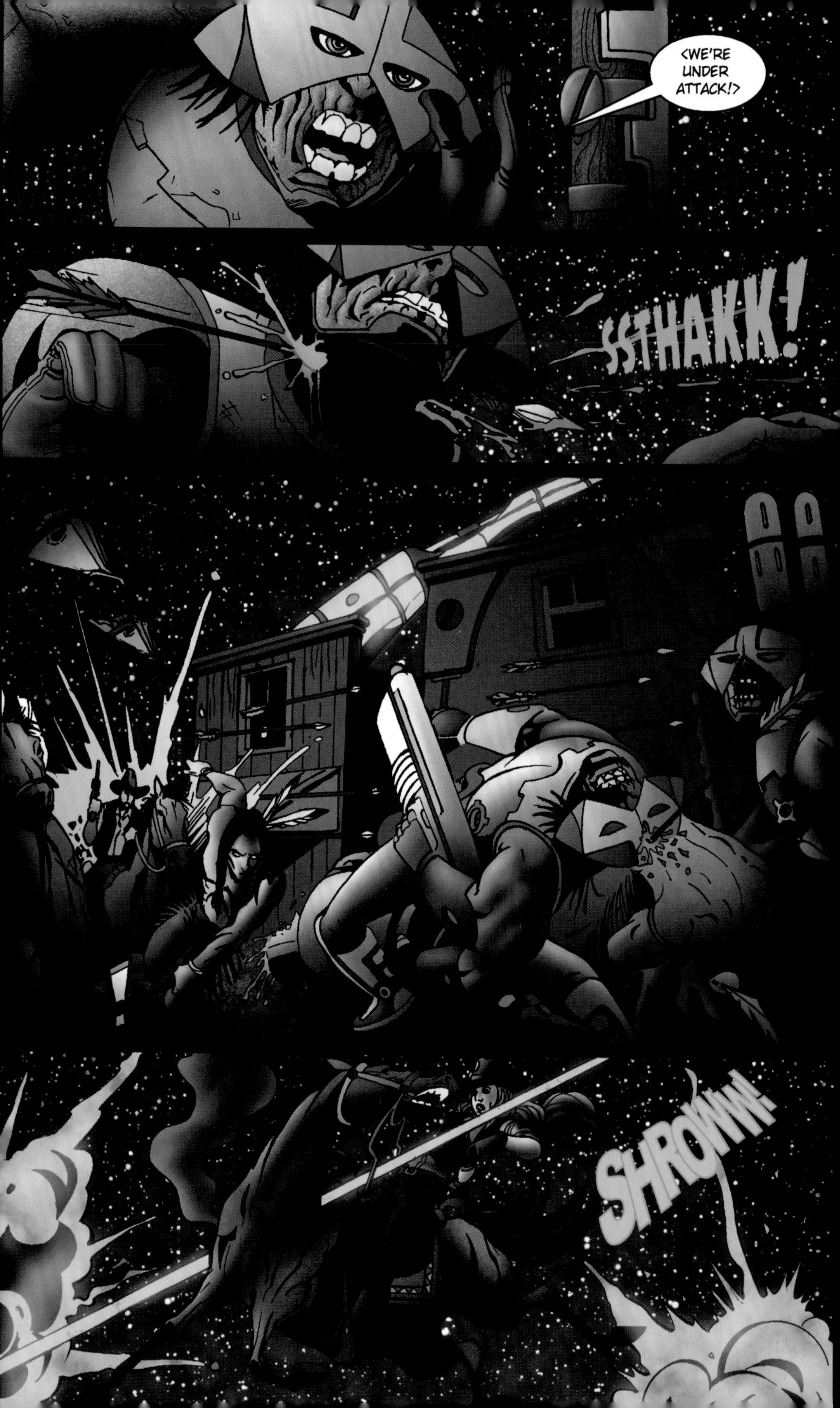
<WE'RE UNDER ATTACK!>
SSTHAKK!
SHROWW!

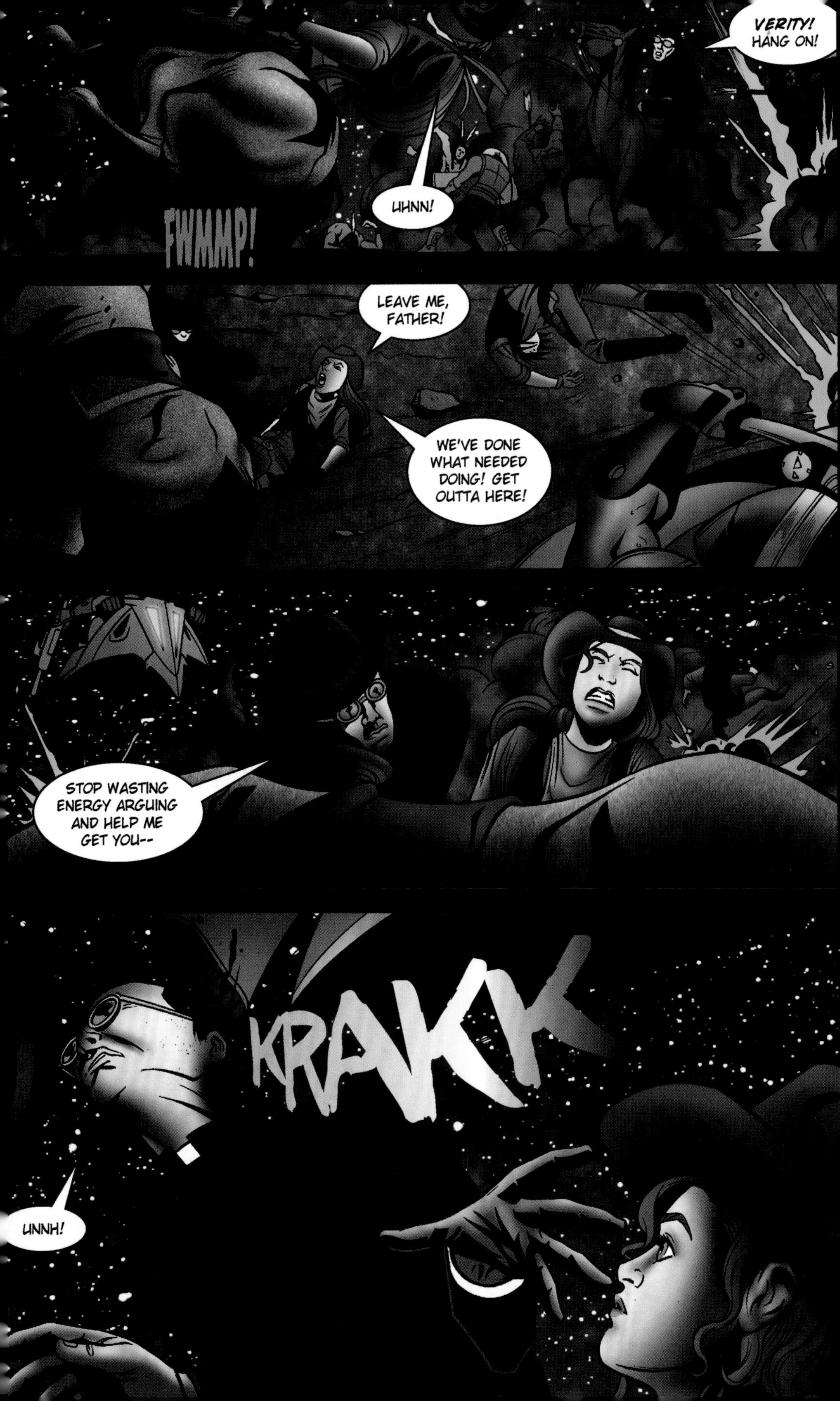
VERITY! HANG ON!
UHNN!
FWMMP!
LEAVE ME, FATHER!
WE'VE DONE WHAT NEEDED DOING! GET OUTTA HERE!
STOP WASTING ENERGY ARGUING AND HELP ME GET YOU--
KRAKK
UNNH!

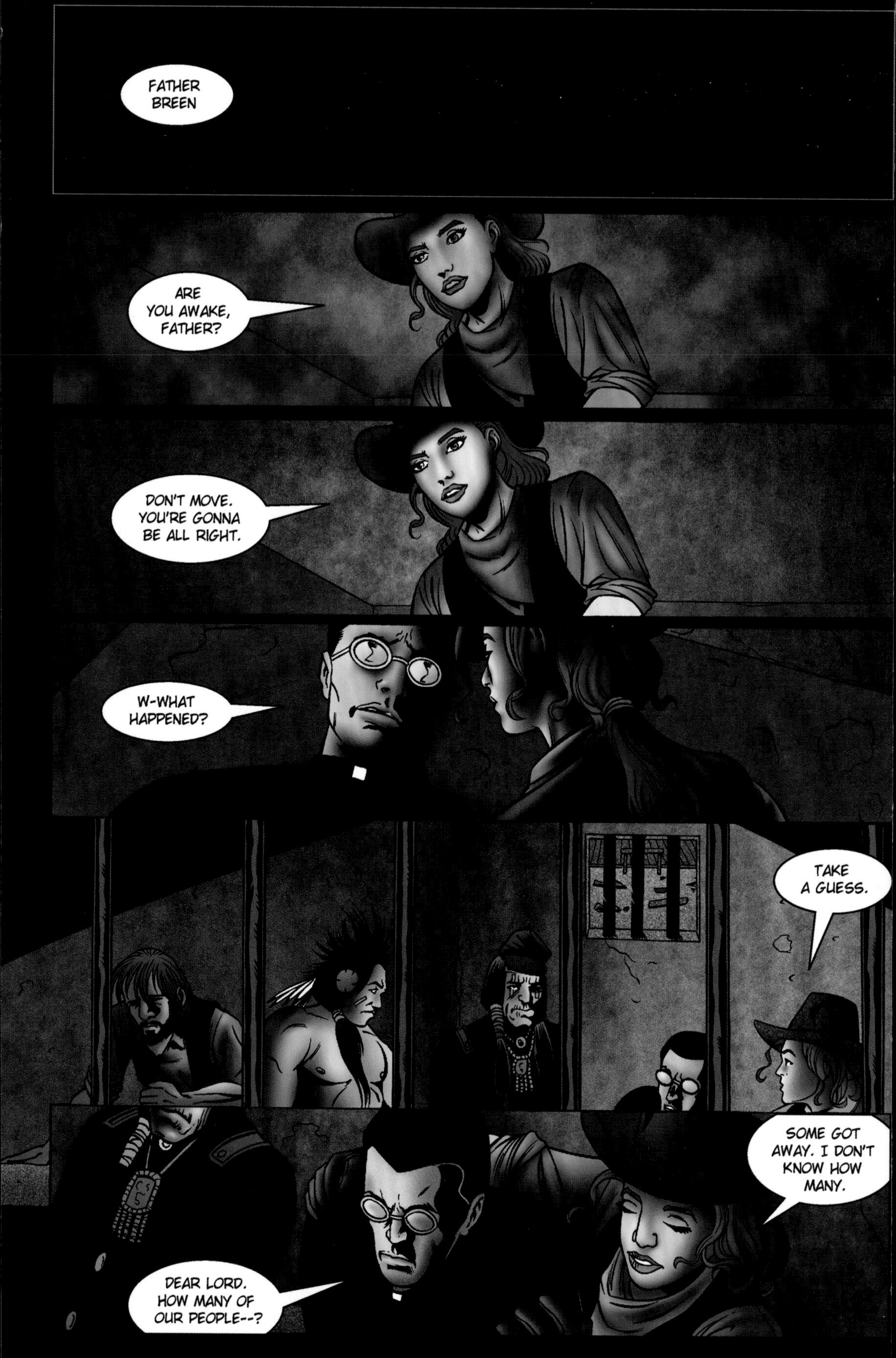
FATHER BREEN
ARE YOU AWAKE, FATHER?
DON'T MOVE. YOU'RE GONNA BE ALL RIGHT.
W-WHAT HAPPENED?
TAKE A GUESS.
SOME GOT AWAY. I DON'T KNOW HOW MANY.
DEAR LORD. HOW MANY OF OUR PEOPLE--?

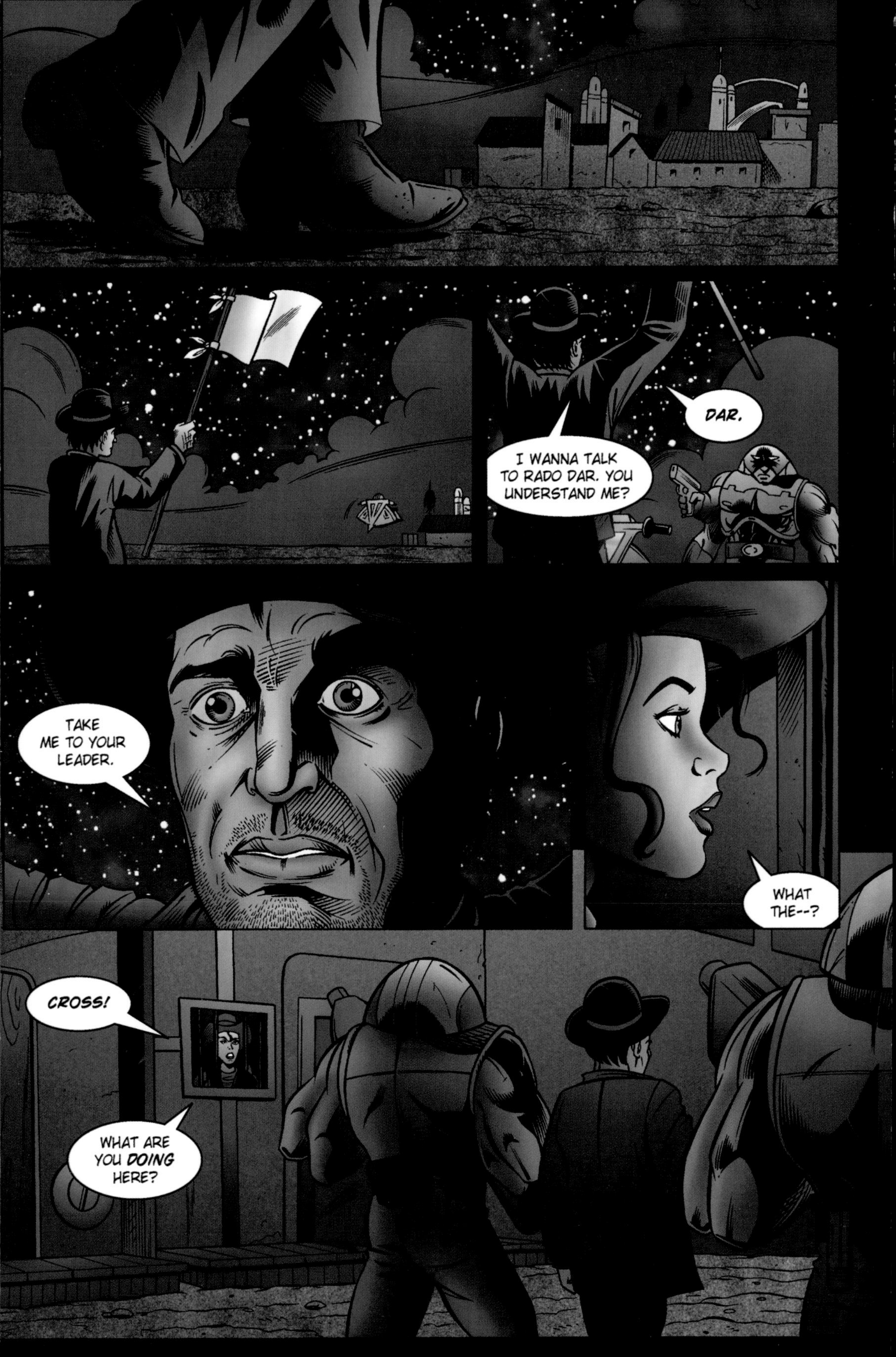
DAR.
I WANNA TALK TO RADO DAR. YOU UNDERSTAND ME?
TAKE ME TO YOUR LEADER.
WHAT THE--?
CROSS!
WHAT ARE YOU **DOING** HERE?

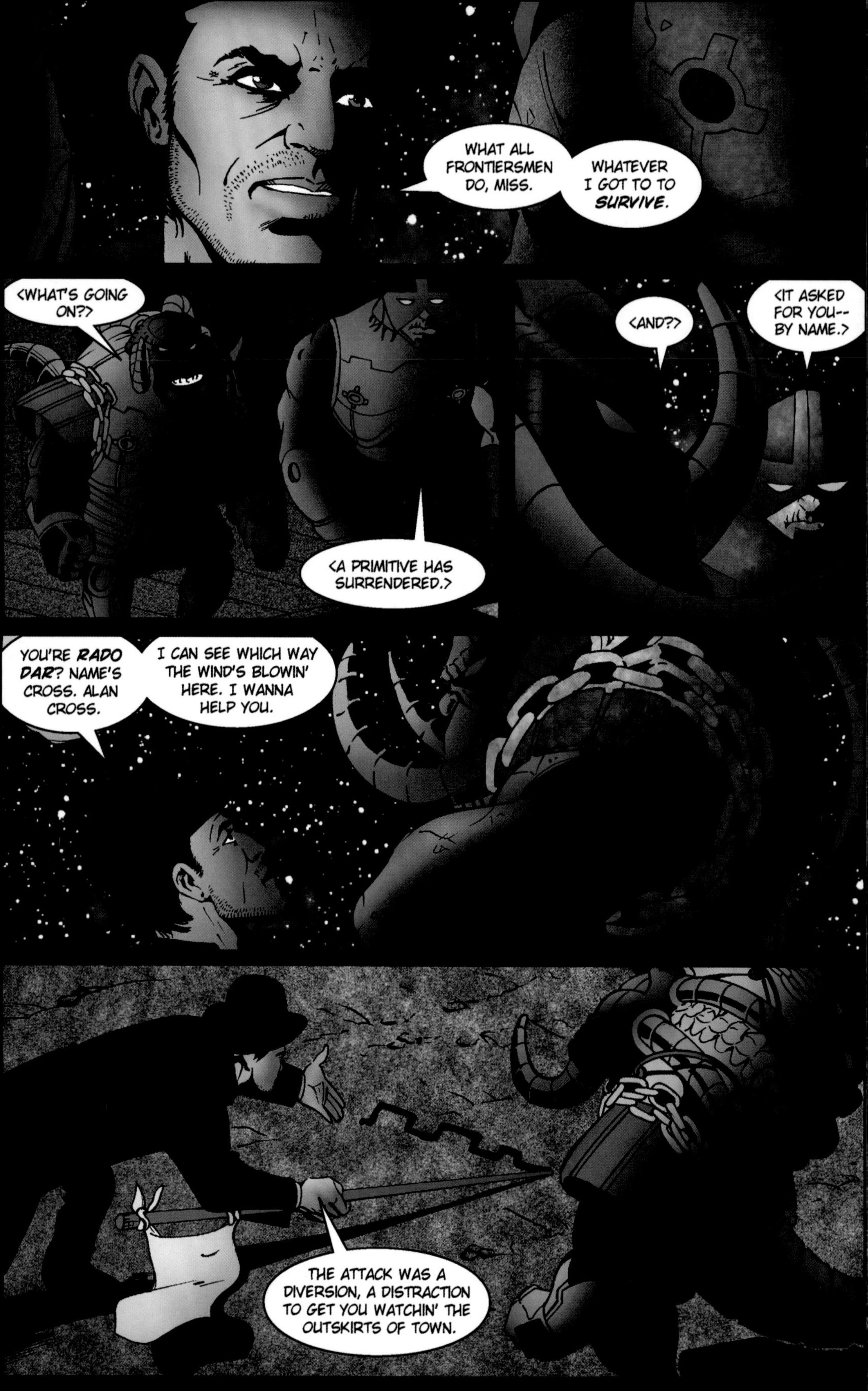
WHAT ALL FRONTIERSMEN DO, MISS.
WHATEVER I GOT TO TO *SURVIVE*.
<WHAT'S GOING ON?>
<A PRIMITIVE HAS SURRENDERED.>
<AND?>
<IT ASKED FOR YOU-- BY NAME.>
YOU'RE *RADO DAR*? NAME'S CROSS. ALAN CROSS.
I CAN SEE WHICH WAY THE WIND'S BLOWIN' HERE. I WANNA HELP YOU.
THE ATTACK WAS A DIVERSION, A DISTRACTION TO GET YOU WATCHIN' THE OUTSKIRTS OF TOWN.

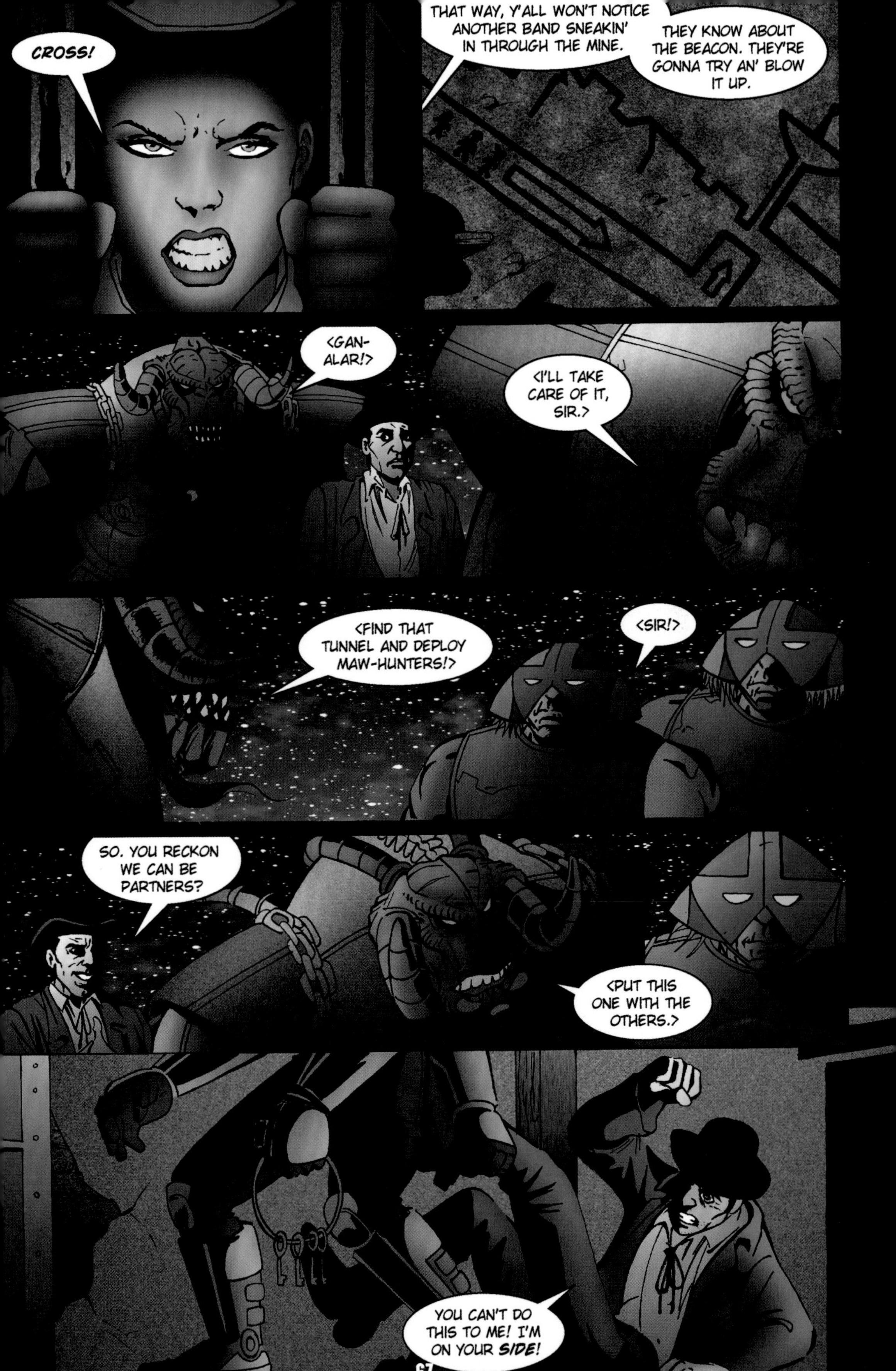
CROSS!
THAT WAY, Y'ALL WON'T NOTICE ANOTHER BAND SNEAKIN' IN THROUGH THE MINE.
THEY KNOW ABOUT THE BEACON. THEY'RE GONNA TRY AN' BLOW IT UP.
<GAN-ALAR!>
<I'LL TAKE CARE OF IT, SIR.>
<FIND THAT TUNNEL AND DEPLOY MAW-HUNTERS!>
<SIR!>
SO. YOU RECKON WE CAN BE PARTNERS?
<PUT THIS ONE WITH THE OTHERS.>
YOU CAN'T DO THIS TO ME! I'M ON YOUR ***SIDE!***

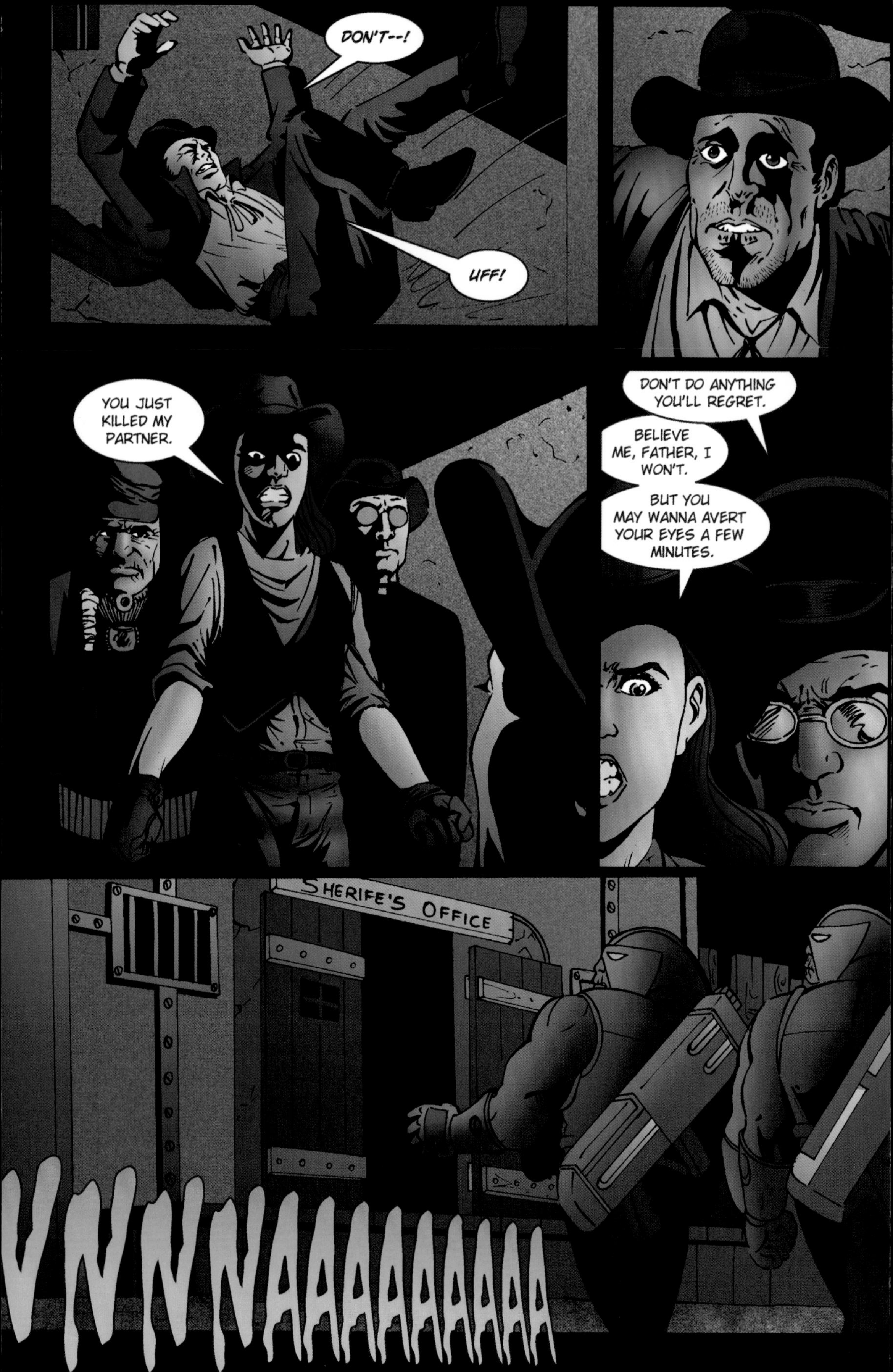
DON'T--!
UFF!
YOU JUST KILLED MY PARTNER.
DON'T DO ANYTHING YOU'LL REGRET.
BELIEVE ME, FATHER, I WON'T.
BUT YOU MAY WANNA AVERT YOUR EYES A FEW MINUTES.
SHERIFE'S OFFICE
VNNNAAAAAAAA

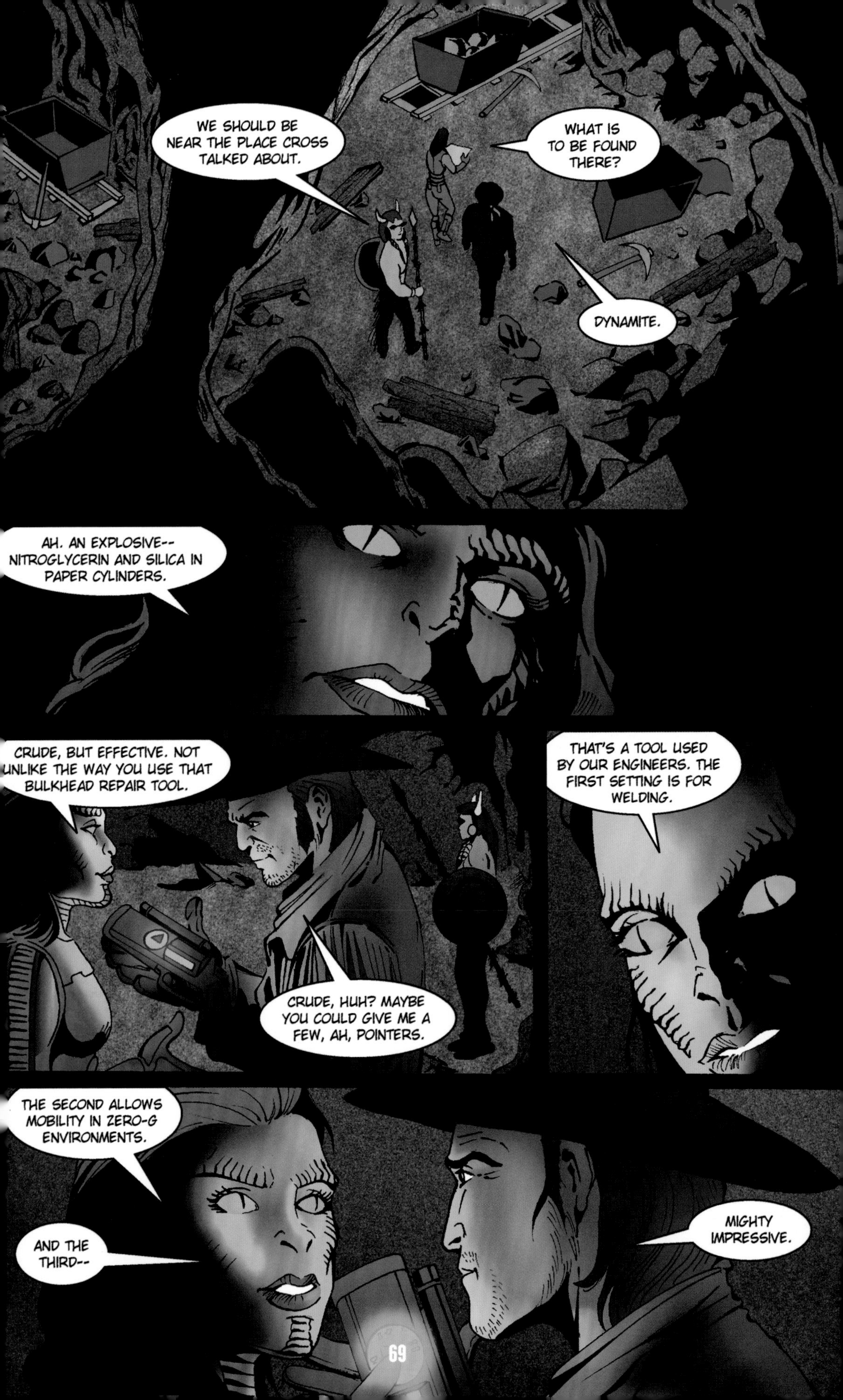

WE SHOULD BE NEAR THE PLACE CROSS TALKED ABOUT.
WHAT IS TO BE FOUND THERE?
DYNAMITE.
AH. AN EXPLOSIVE-- NITROGLYCERIN AND SILICA IN PAPER CYLINDERS.
CRUDE, BUT EFFECTIVE. NOT UNLIKE THE WAY YOU USE THAT BULKHEAD REPAIR TOOL.
CRUDE, HUH? MAYBE YOU COULD GIVE ME A FEW, AH, POINTERS.
THAT'S A TOOL USED BY OUR ENGINEERS. THE FIRST SETTING IS FOR WELDING.
THE SECOND ALLOWS MOBILITY IN ZERO-G ENVIRONMENTS.
AND THE THIRD--
MIGHTY IMPRESSIVE.

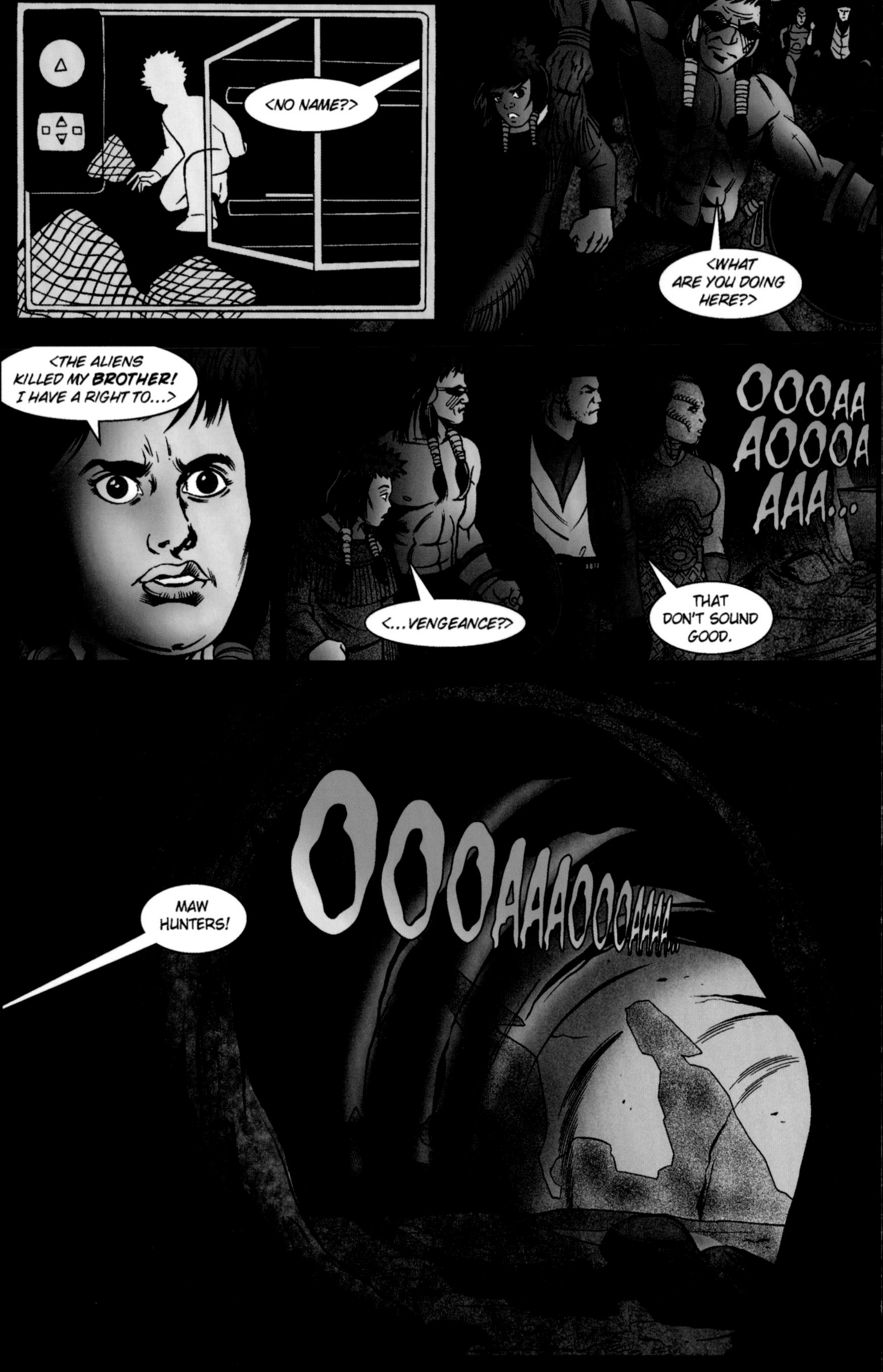
<NO NAME?>
<WHAT ARE YOU DOING HERE?>
<THE ALIENS KILLED MY **BROTHER!** I HAVE A RIGHT TO...>
<...VENGEANCE?>
OOOAA AOOOA AAA...
THAT DON'T SOUND GOOD.
MAW HUNTERS!
OOOAAAOOOAAAA...

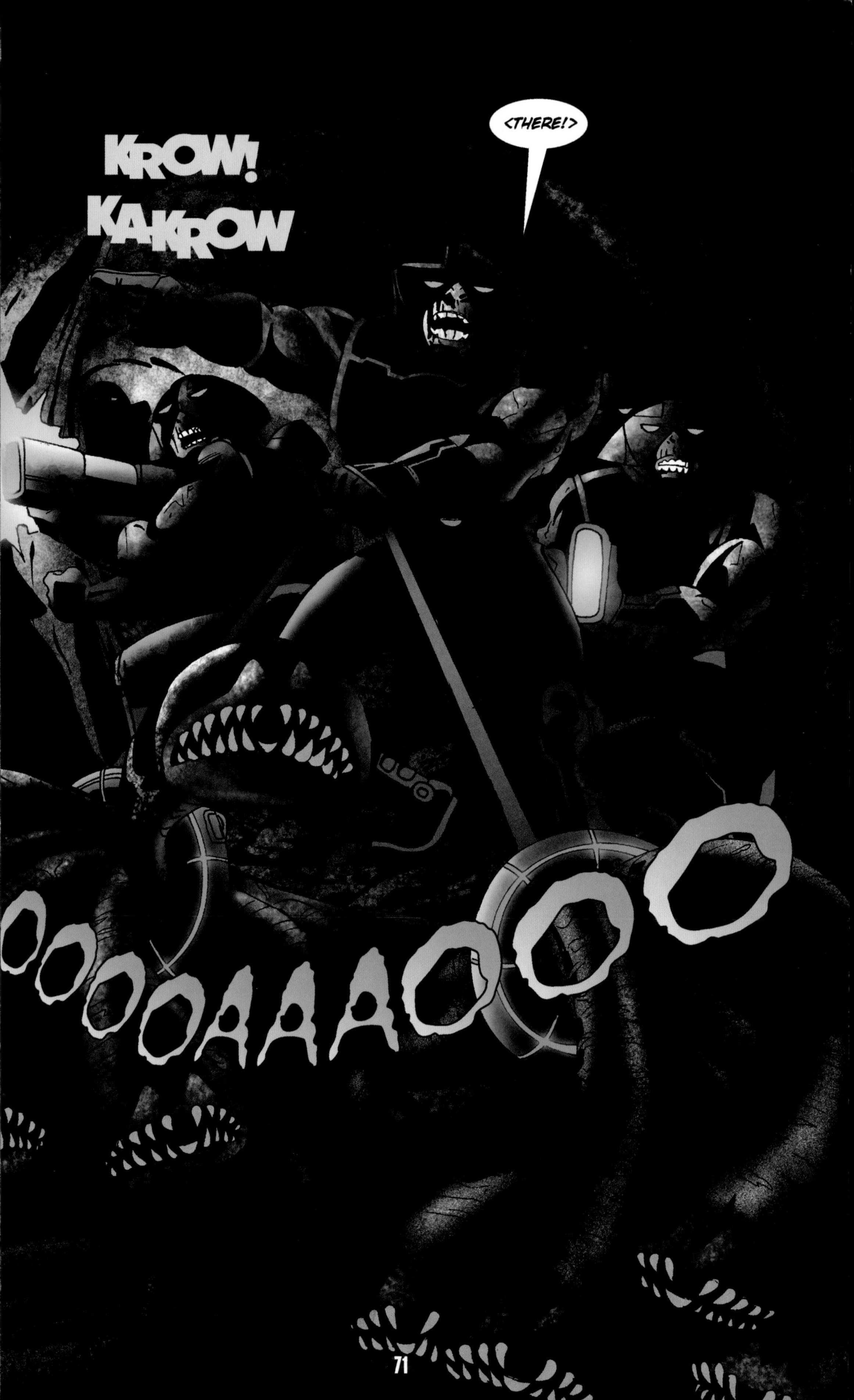
KROW!
KA-KROW
<THERE!>
OOOOOAAAAOOOOO

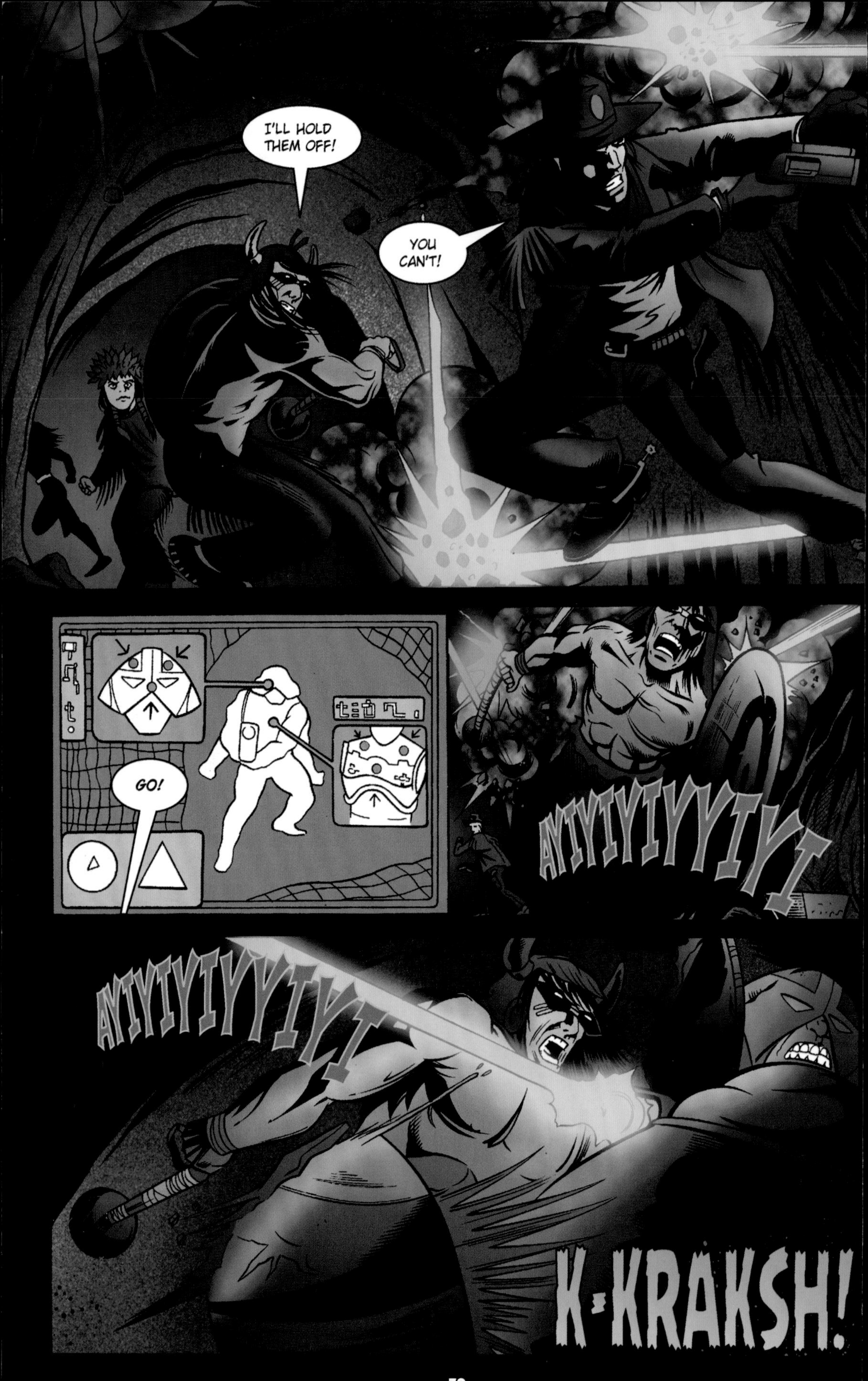
I'LL HOLD THEM OFF!
YOU CAN'T!
GO!
AYIYIYIYYIYI
AYIYIYIYYIYI
K-KRAKSH!

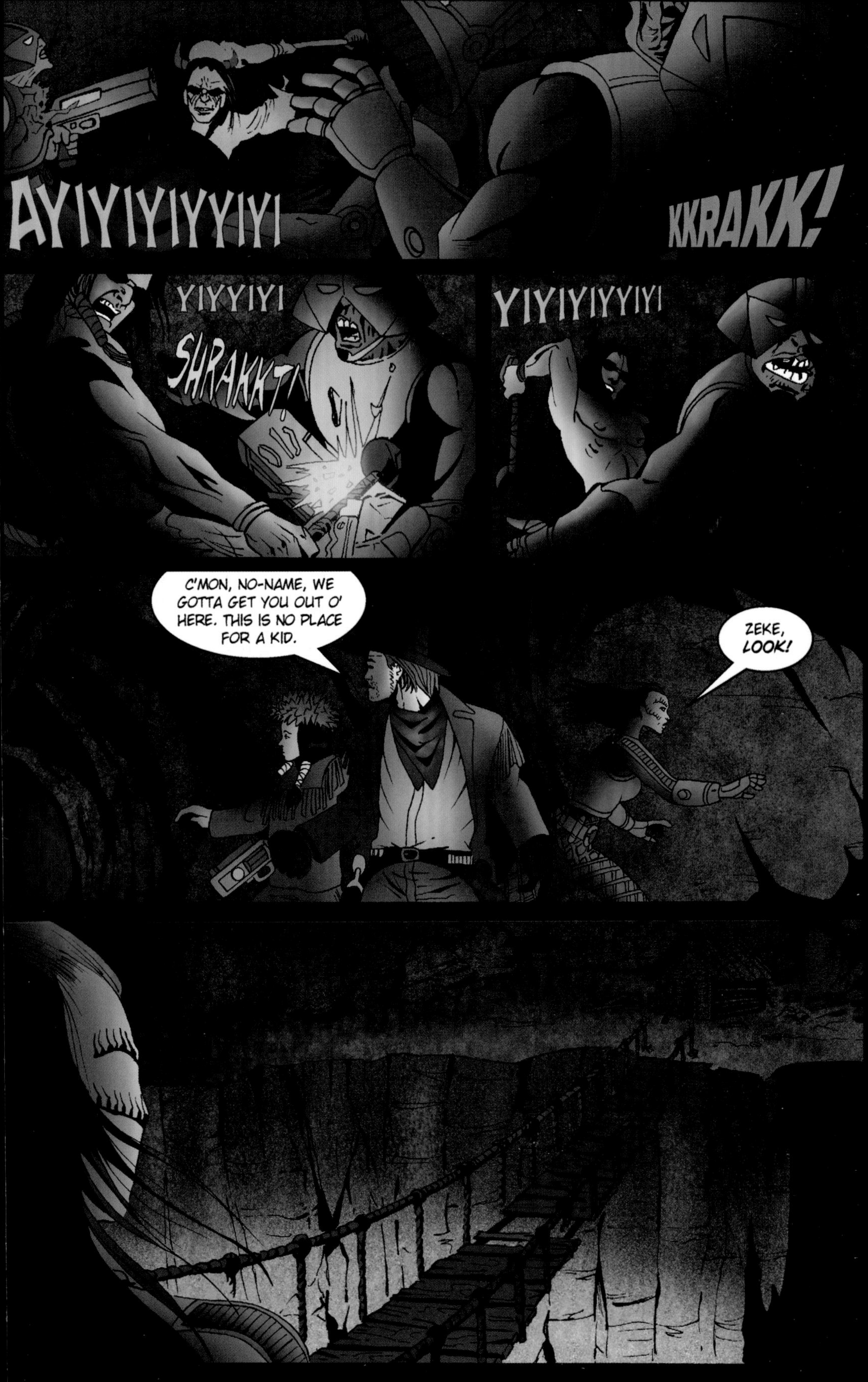
AYIYIYIYYIYI
KKRAKK!
YIYYIYI
SHRAKKT!
YIYIYIYYIYI
C'MON, NO-NAME, WE GOTTA GET YOU OUT O' HERE. THIS IS NO PLACE FOR A KID.
ZEKE, LOOK!

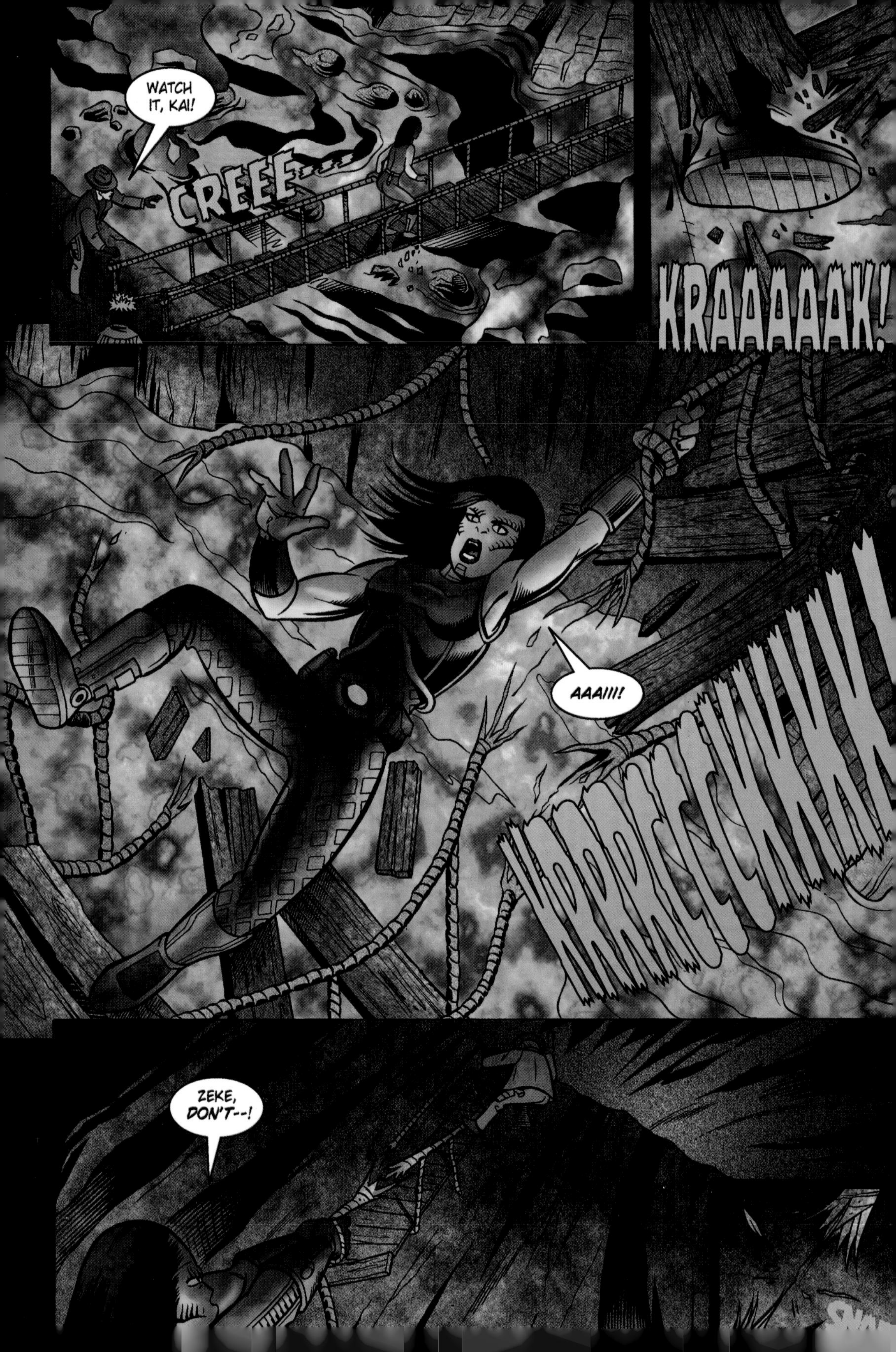
WATCH IT, KAI!
CREEE...
KRAAAAAK!
AAAIII!
ZEKE, DON'T--!

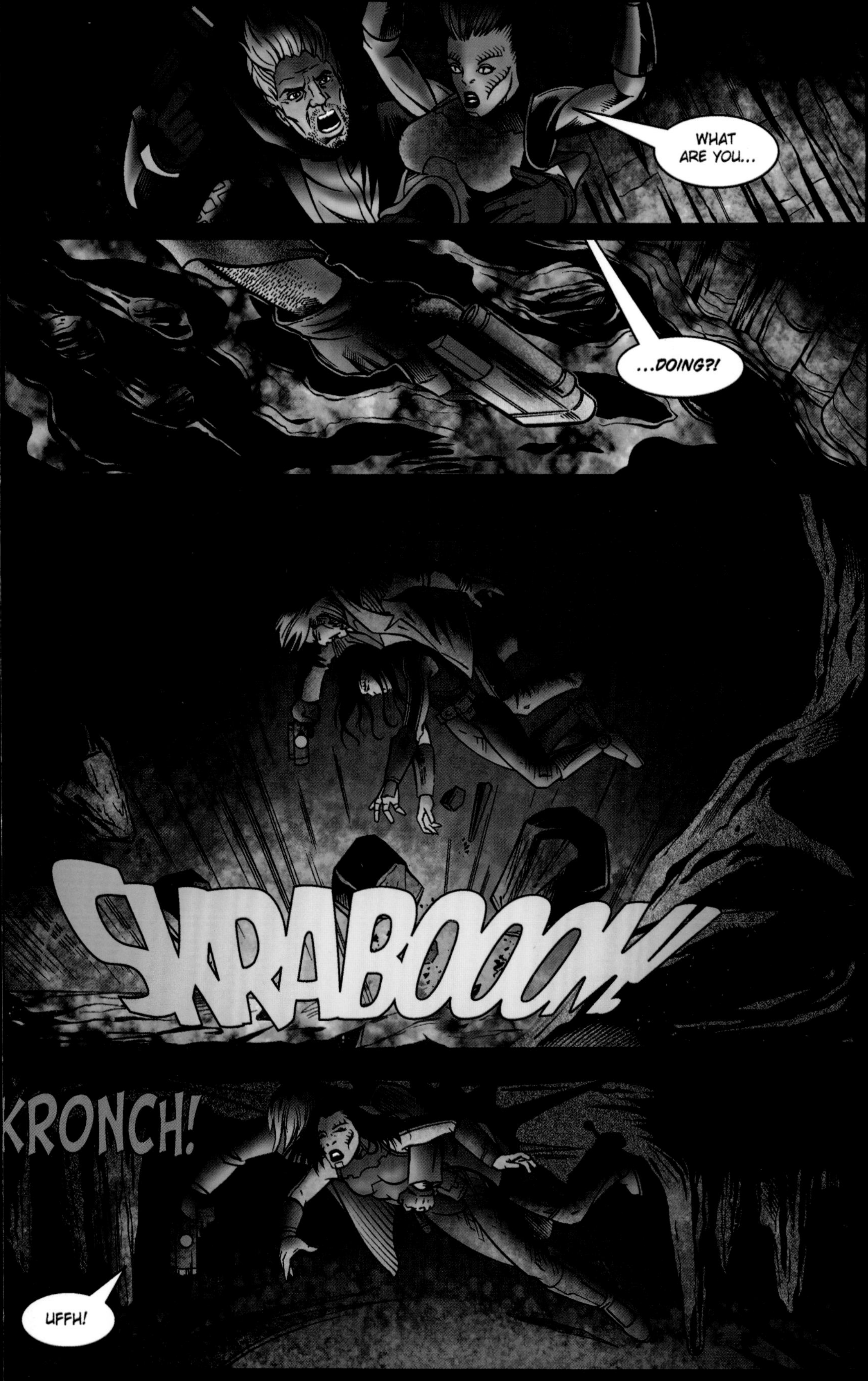
WHAT ARE YOU...
...DOING?!
SKRABOOOM!
KRONCH!
UFFH!

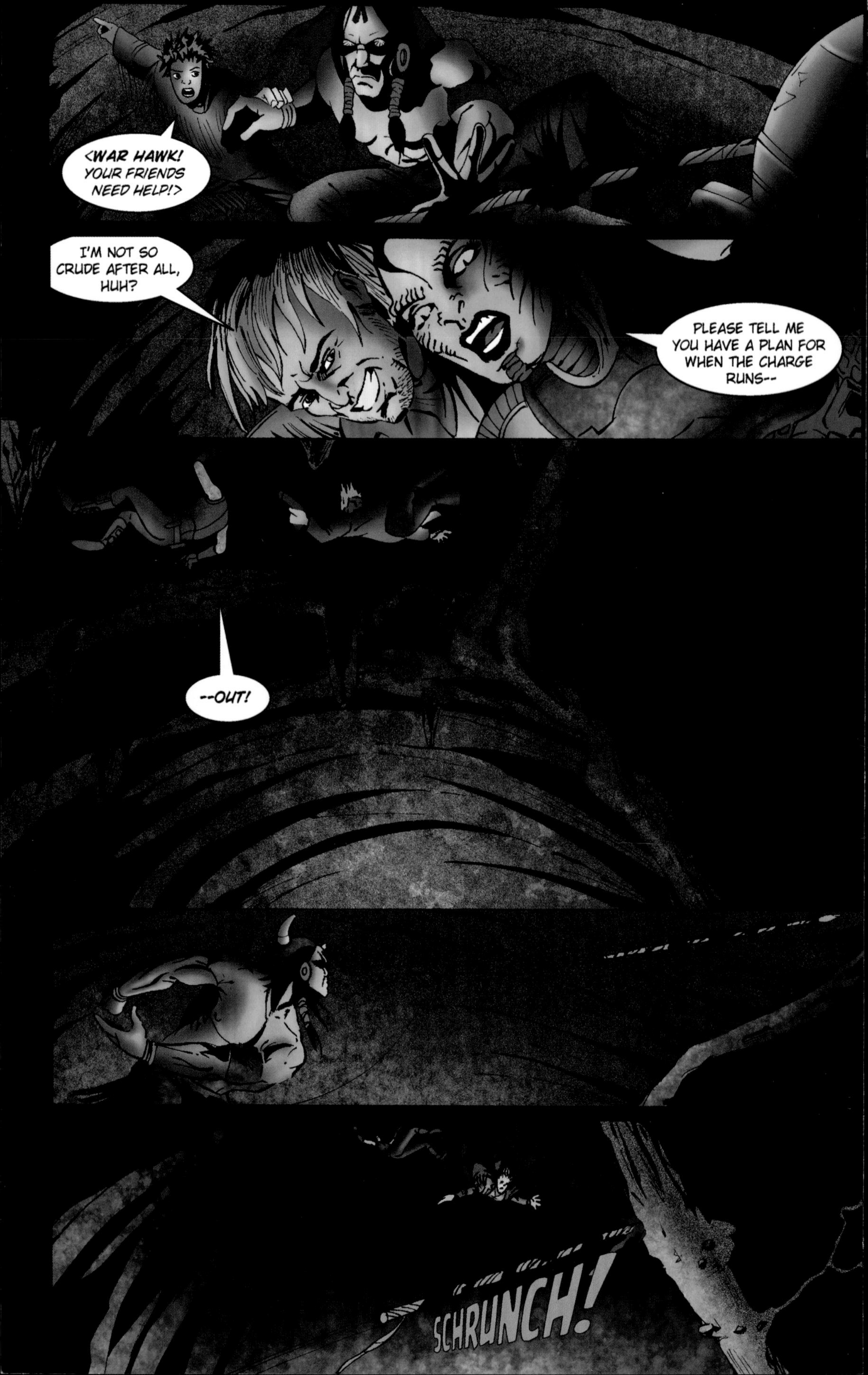
<WAR HAWK! YOUR FRIENDS NEED HELP!>
I'M NOT SO CRUDE AFTER ALL, HUH?
PLEASE TELL ME YOU HAVE A PLAN FOR WHEN THE CHARGE RUNS--
--OUT!
SCHRUNCH!

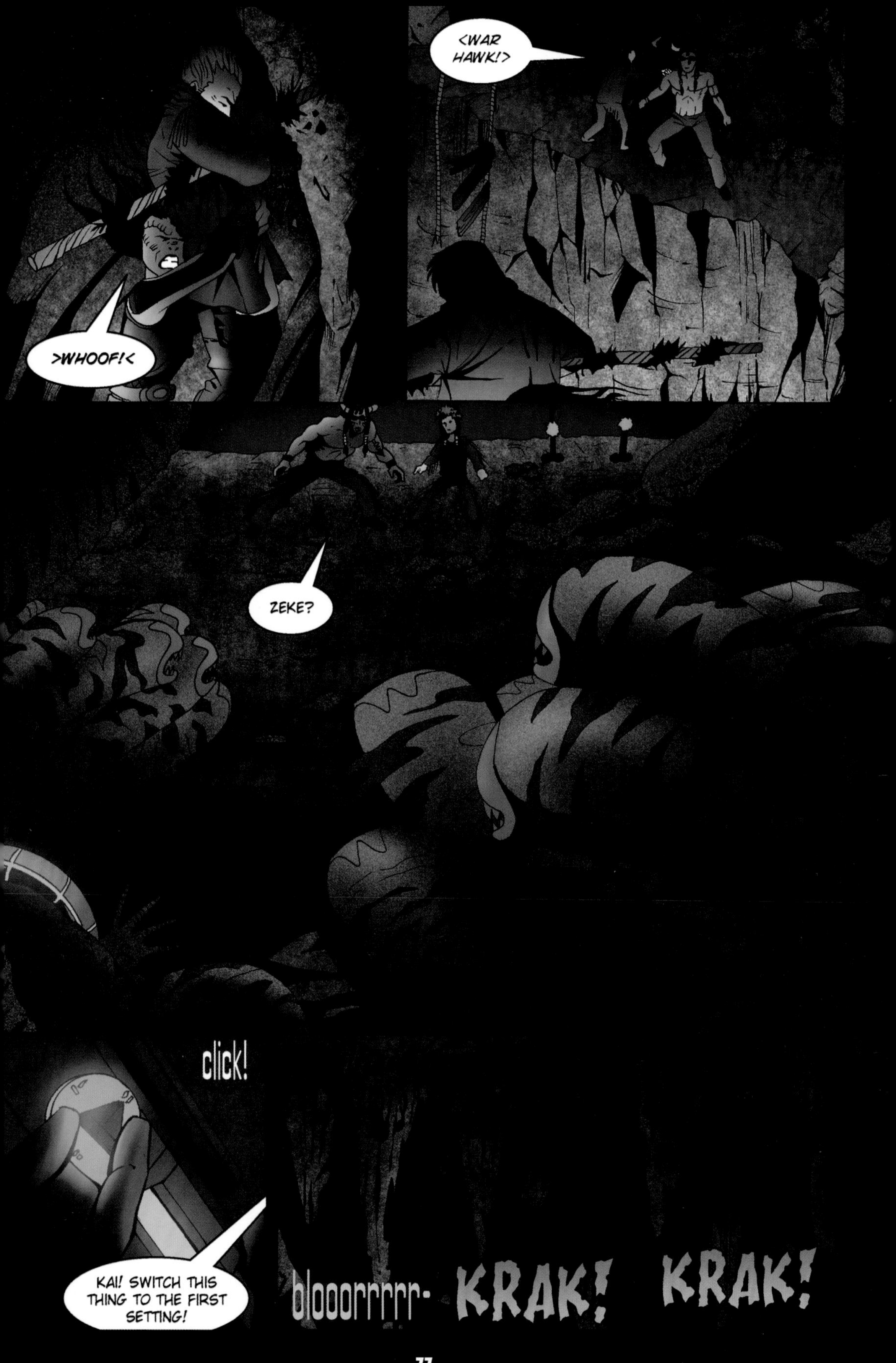
>WHOOF!<
<WAR HAWK!>
ZEKE?
click!
KAI! SWITCH THIS THING TO THE FIRST SETTING!
bloorrrrr-
KRAK!
KRAK!

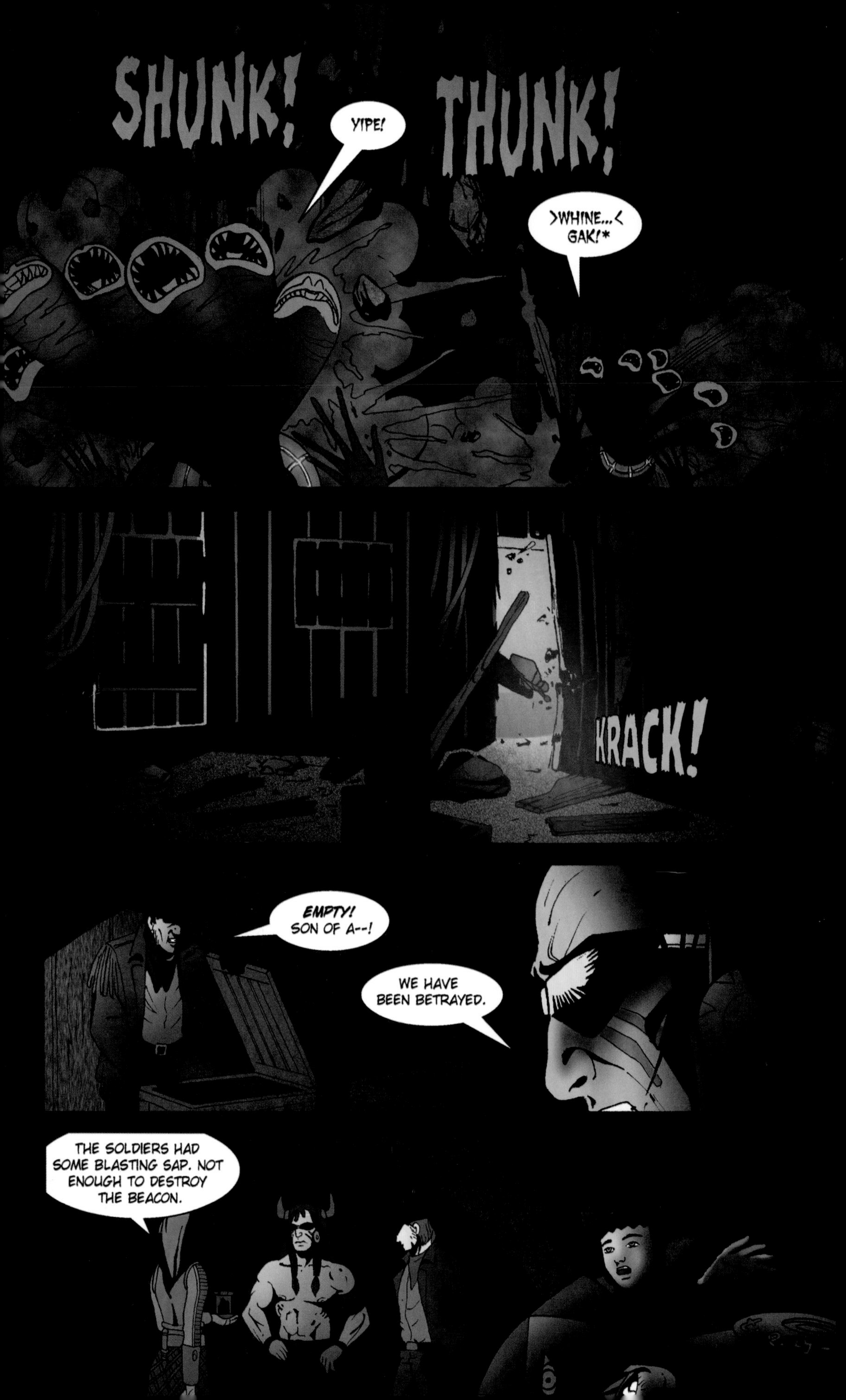
SHUNK!
YIPE!
THUNK!
>WHINE...< GAK!*
KRACK!
EMPTY! SON OF A--!
WE HAVE BEEN BETRAYED.
THE SOLDIERS HAD SOME BLASTING SAP. NOT ENOUGH TO DESTROY THE BEACON.

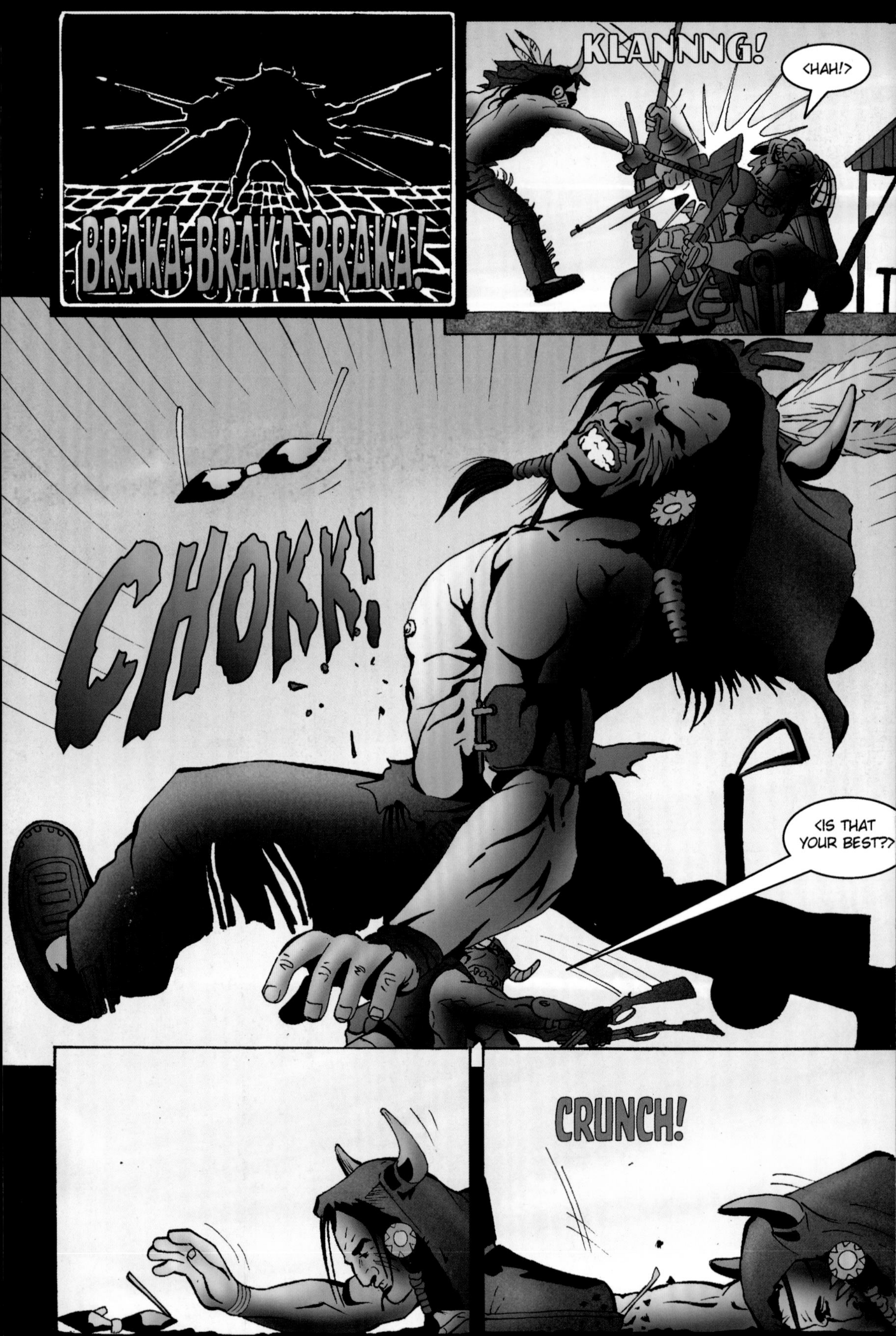
BRAKA-BRAKA-BRAKA!
KLANNNG!
<HAH!>
CHOKK!
<IS THAT YOUR BEST?>
CRUNCH!

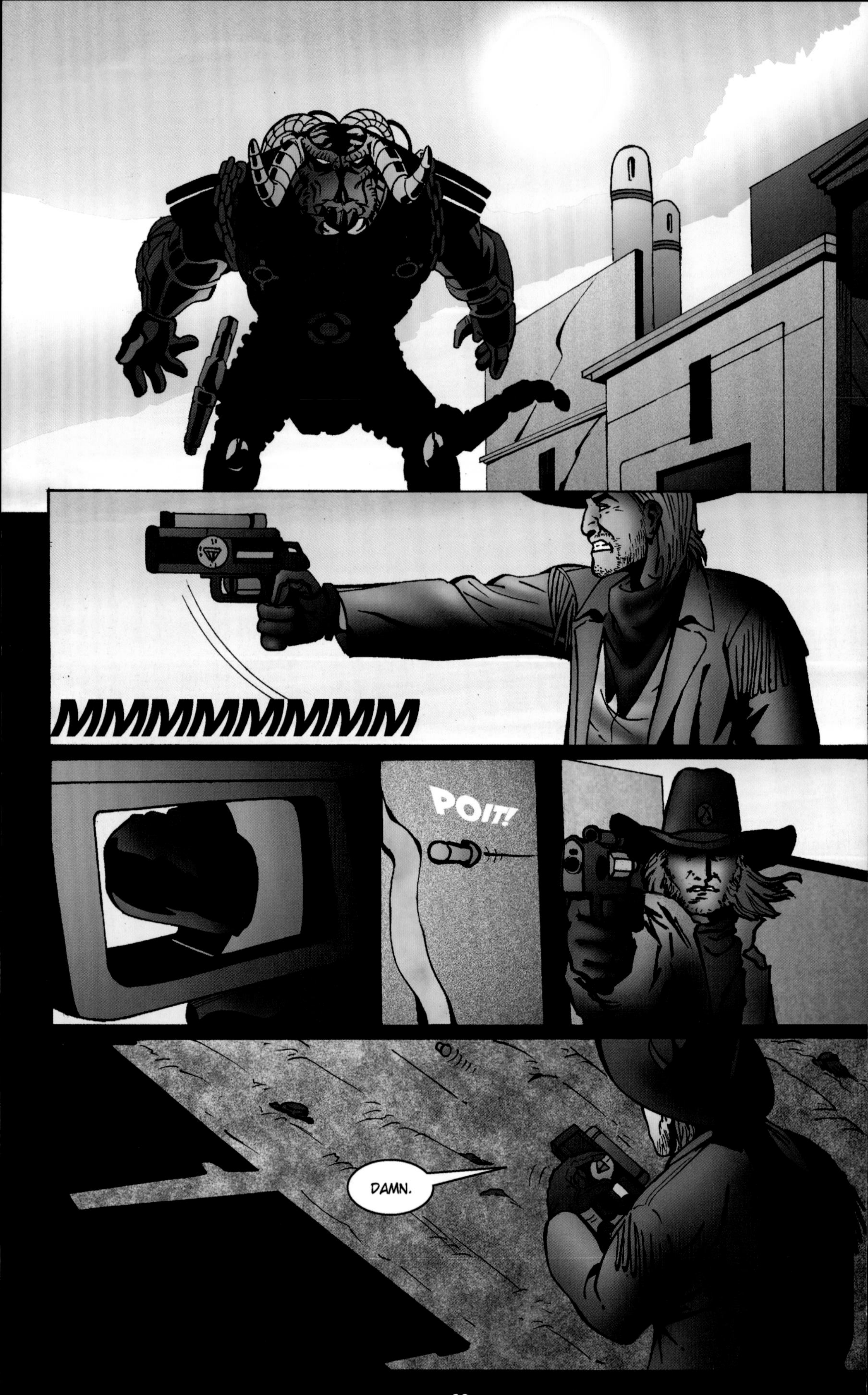
MMMMMMMMM
POIT!
DAMN.

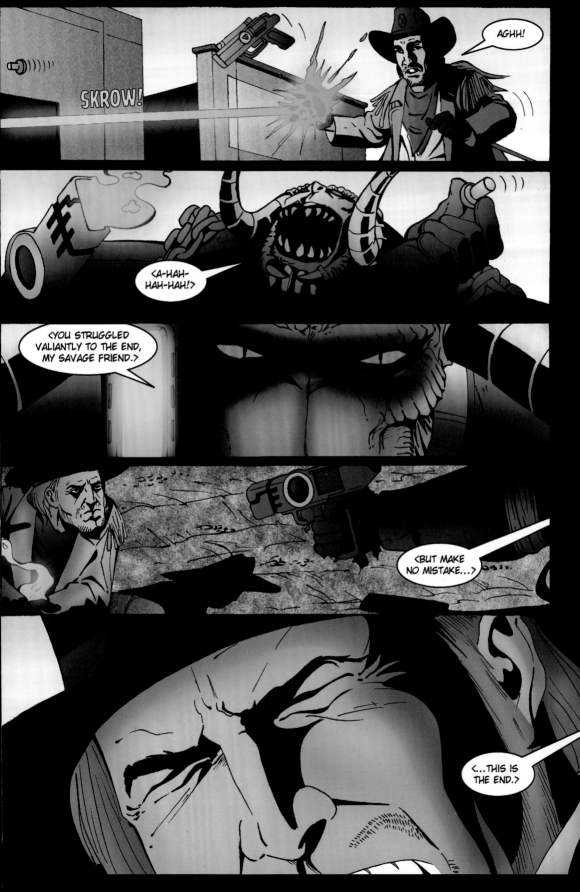

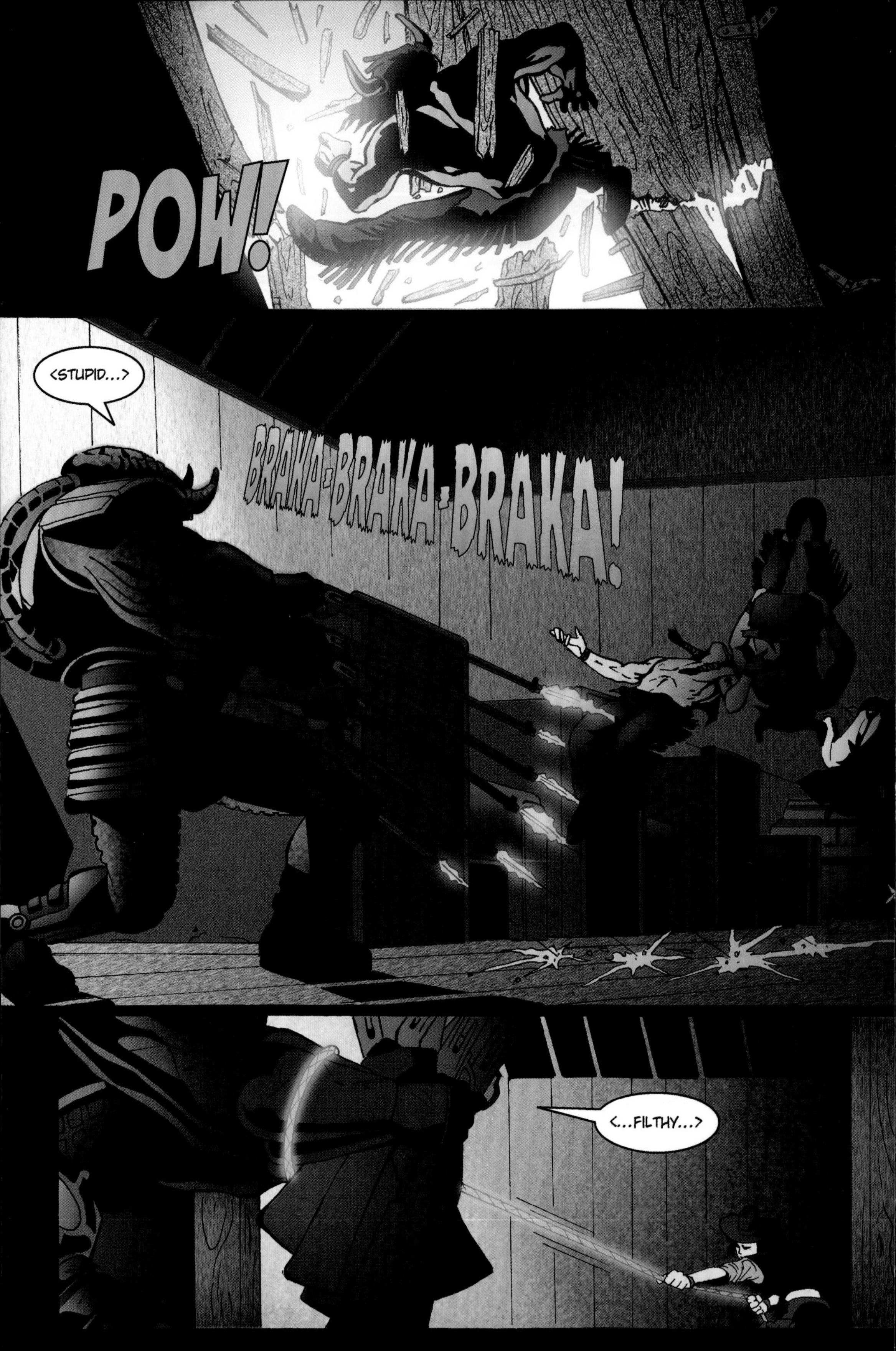
POW!
<STUPID...>
BRAKA-BRAKA-BRAKA!
<...FILTHY...>

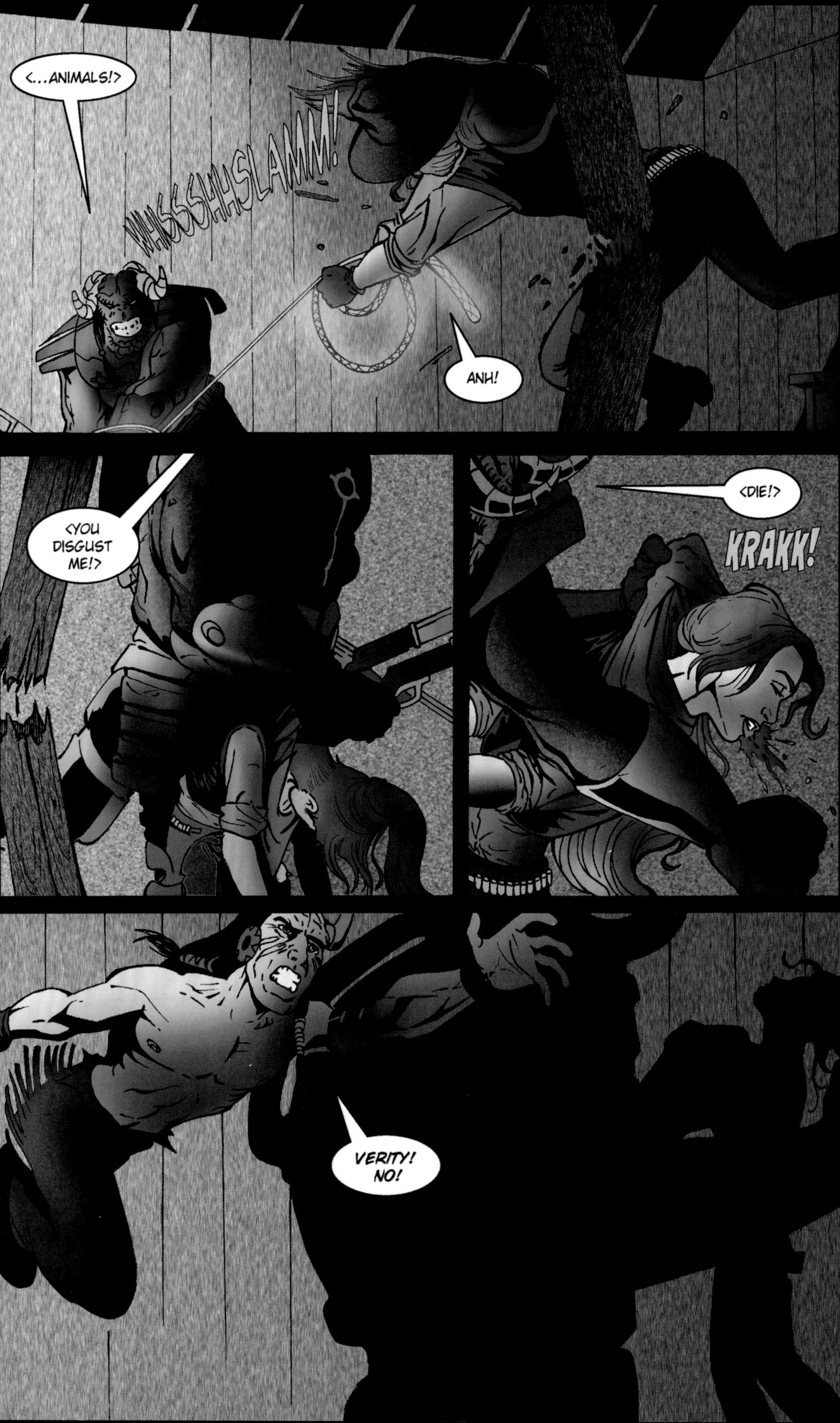
<...ANIMALS!>
WHSSSHHSLAMM!
ANH!
<YOU DISGUST ME!>
<DIE!>
KRAKK!
VERITY! NO!

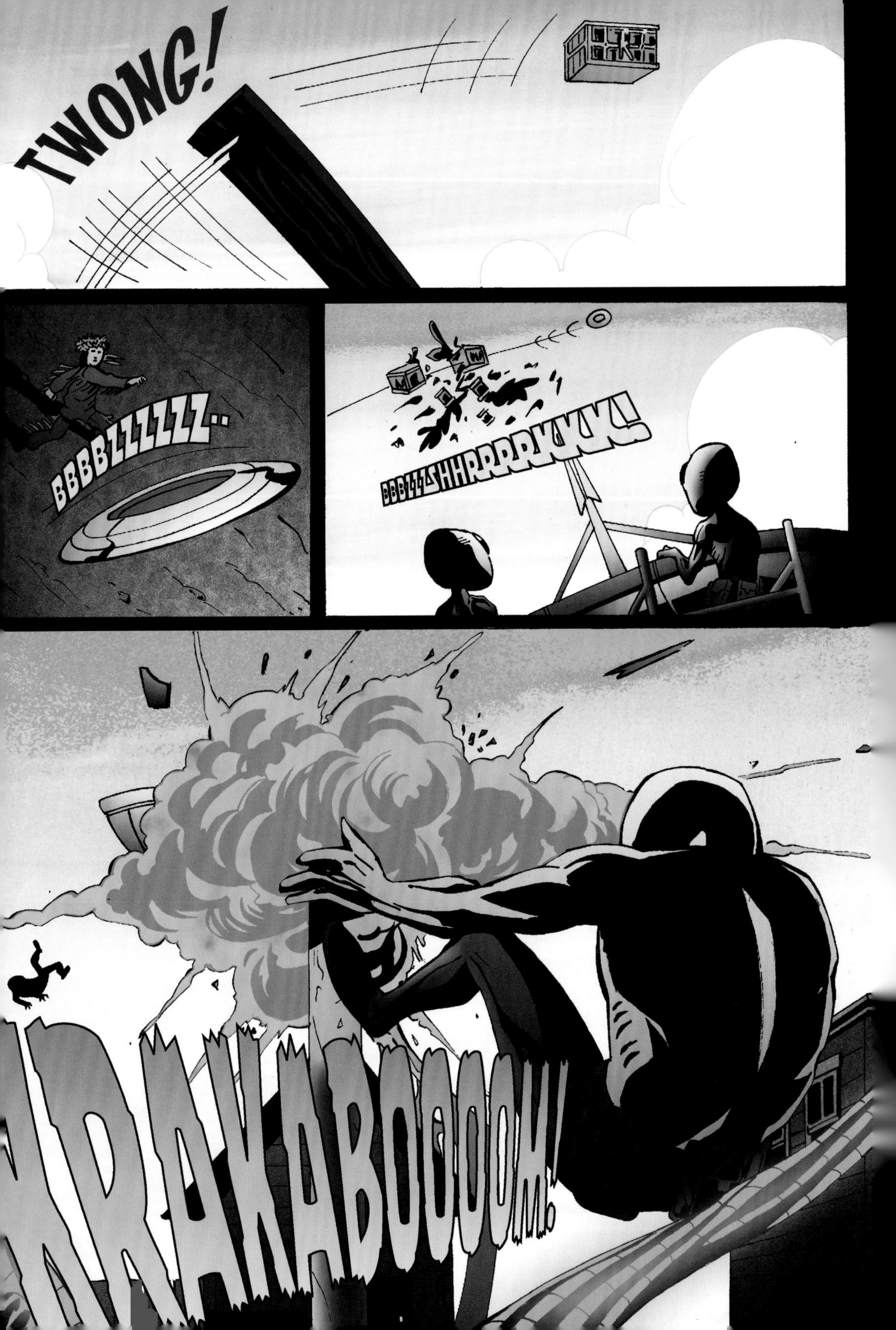
TWONG!
BBBBZZZZZZ..
BBBZZZSHHRRRRKKKK!
RAKABOOOOM!

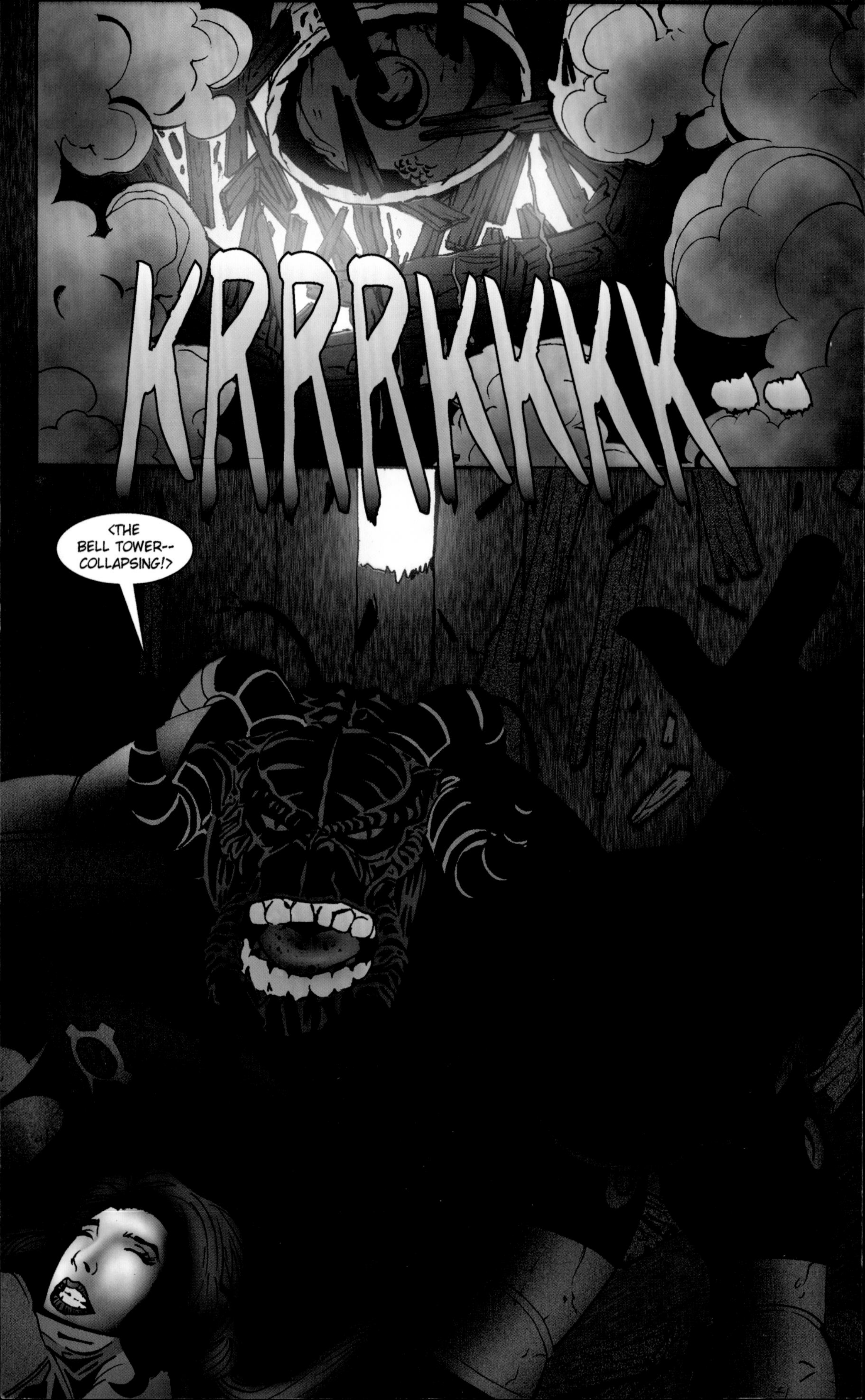
KRRRKKKKK--
<THE BELL TOWER-- COLLAPSING!>

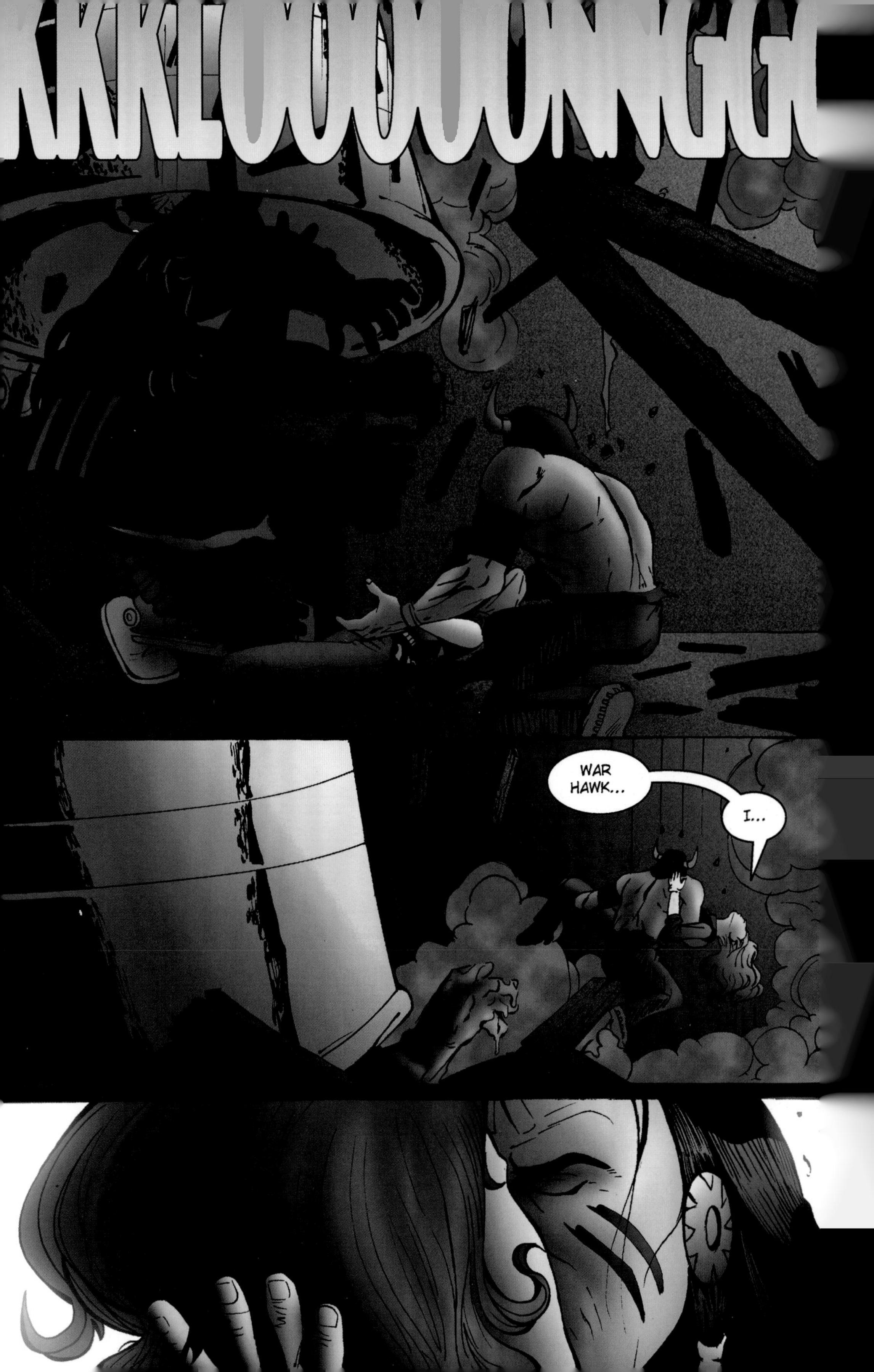
KKKLOOOOONNGG
WAR HAWK...
I...

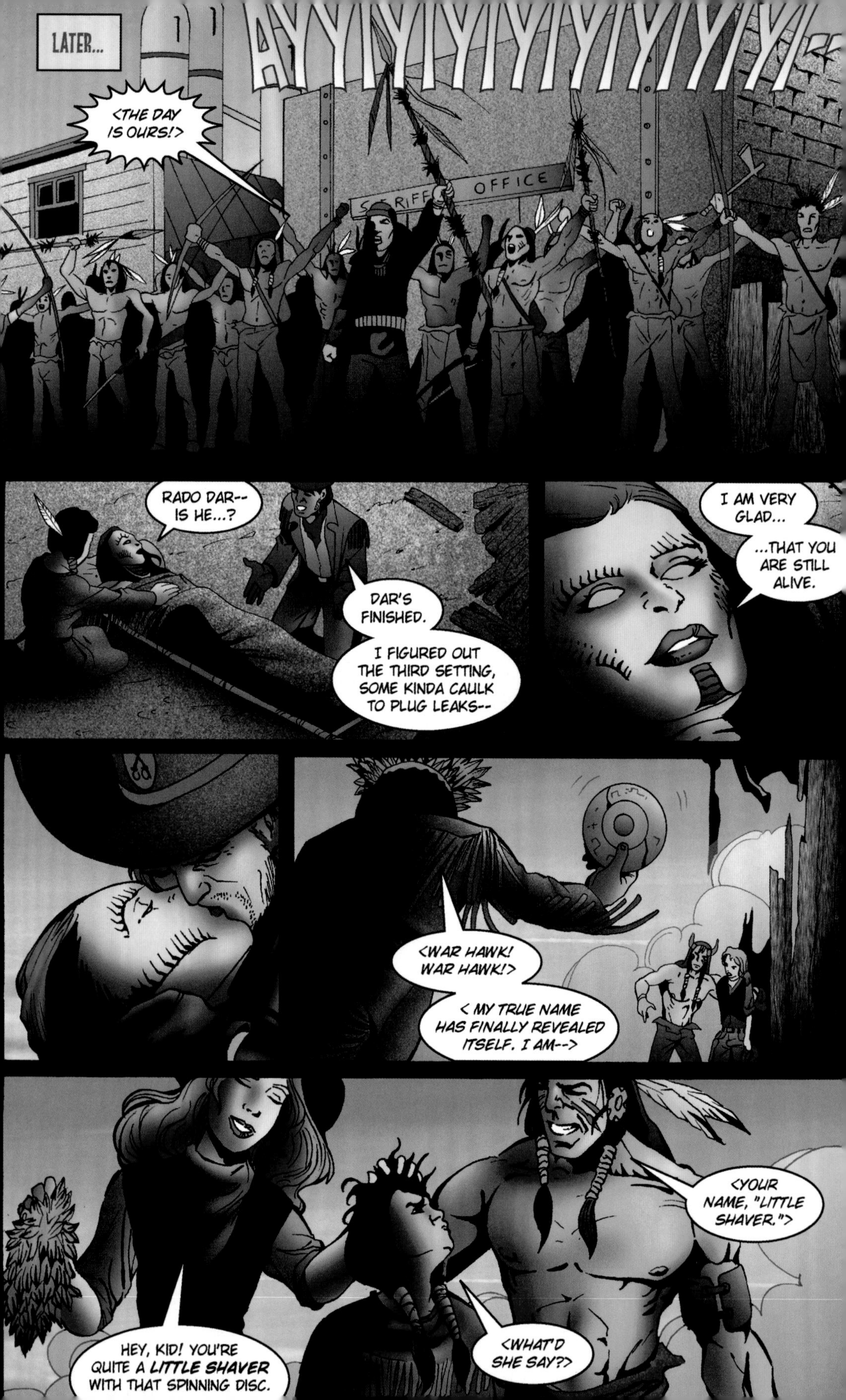
LATER...
AYYYYYYYYYYY
<THE DAY IS OURS!>
OFFICE
RADO DAR-- IS HE...?
DAR'S FINISHED.
I FIGURED OUT THE THIRD SETTING, SOME KINDA CAULK TO PLUG LEAKS--
I AM VERY GLAD...
...THAT YOU ARE STILL ALIVE.
<WAR HAWK! WAR HAWK!>
< MY TRUE NAME HAS FINALLY REVEALED ITSELF. I AM-->
HEY, KID! YOU'RE QUITE A LITTLE SHAVER WITH THAT SPINNING DISC.
<WHAT'D SHE SAY??>
<YOUR NAME, "LITTLE SHAVER.">

COWBOYS & ALIENS®

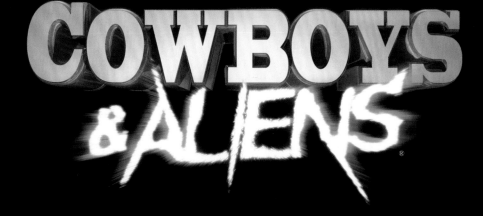

Biographies

Created by: Scott Mitchell Rosenberg

Scott Rosenberg is the chairman of Platinum Studios, Inc., and a producer on the filmed version of his graphic novel creation, *Cowboys & Aliens*.

Scott began his career in the comic book industry at the age of thirteen with a mail-order company to sell comics to make money to be able to buy the comics he wanted. Scott became known for picking early hits from unknown writers and creators. After college, he started his own independent publishing company, Malibu Comics. His first launch, Ex-Mutants, was an instant hit, and Malibu became a leading independent comic book publisher during the comic book heyday of the late 1980s and early 1990s. He developed several industry game-changing paradigms including the computer color standard utilizing Adobe's Photoshop software and artist free-agency when he brokered a deal for several of the top-selling artists to defect from Marvel Comics and form Image Studios with a publishing deal at Malibu—all the while, breaking independent sales records in the industry. One of the new creators whom Scott discovered was Lowell Cunningham, the creator of *Men in Black*, whose work was rejected by more than seventy different publishers. Scott went on to broker the rights deal with Sony Pictures that led to *Men in Black* becoming the billion-dollar franchise it is today. Scott sold Malibu Comics to Marvel Comics in 1994.

In 1996 Scott launched Platinum Studios with the plan of building one of the largest and best libraries of comic book characters in the world, and of bringing together the greatest of comic book and graphic novel talent to develop these characters into all storytelling formats. Since then, Scott has scoured the world for rights to great comic book characters, in addition to creating them as part of the Platinum Studios Macroverse—a unique universe of characters that spans billions of years and multiple dimensions. *Cowboys & Aliens* hails from the Platinum Studios Macroverse. Scott and the Platinum Studios team continue to look for exciting material with stories that need to be told, including through Platinum Studios' Comic Book Challenge™—an *American Idol*–inspired competition for comic book creators around the world. Platinum Studios library includes thousands of characters that have been published in millions of books around the world. Today Scott creates, produces, and develops comic book properties for all media. His vision has allowed Platinum Studios to develop the business model of the future, where properties are developed simultaneously for multiple distribution models, maximizing profitability, visibility, and availability for everyone involved from the creator to the consumer.

Scott has been happily married since 1992 and lives in California with the three loves of his life: his wife and two daughters.

Writer: Fred Van Lente

Fred Van Lente is the #1 *New York Times* bestselling author of Incredible Hercules (with Greg Pak) and three entries in the Marvel Zombies series, as well as the American Library Association award-winning Action Philosophers. Van Lente's other comics include Comic Book Comics, MODOK's 11, X Men Noir, and Amazing Spider-Man.

Writer: Andrew Foley

Andrew Foley attended the Alberta College of Art in Calgary, Alberta, where he still lives with his wife, Tiina. Andrew is writing a variety of other comics and graphic novels for Platinum Studios, including Conviction, Age of Kings, and *Return of the Wraith*. His other comics work includes *Parting Ways*, a 142-page graphic novel illustrated by Scott Mooney and Nick

Creator Bios

Pencils: Luciano Lima

Luciano Lima is a comics artist living in São Paolo, Brazil, where he is part of Fabricio Grellet's Magic Eye Studios. He has worked for Dark Horse on Grifter and The Mask, for Marvel on Wolverine and X-Force, and for the French publisher Semic.

Inks: Luciano Kars & J. Wilson

Kars and Wilson are both staff artists at Brazil's Magic Eye Studios, a comics art and script studio managed by Fabricio Grellet that has produced work for comic book and graphic novel publishers around the world.

Inks: Silvio Spotti

Silvio Spotti was born in São Paulo, where he still lives and works. He has a degree in arts from the FMU/FAAM university, and began his career in 1992 as a penciller for the small press in Brazil. In 1996 he started working as an inker, working on a Brazilian version of the Street Fighter comic book, through the Arthur Garcia Studio. In 2003 he did his first U.S. work through Magic Eye Studios, inking IDW's Wynonna Earp. Since then, he has inked Stargate SG1, Robocop, and Stargate Atlantis for Avatar Press, as well as Daniel Prophet of Dreams for Alias Comics. As a penciller/inker, Spotti has also done work for Disney (USA/Europe), drawing stories for Donald Duck, Kim Possible, Toy Story, Little Mermaid, and others.

Color: Andy Elder

Andy Elder began working professionally in comics in 2005. His other credits include inking and coloring Warhead from AIT/Planet Lar, assisting colorists Jamie Grant and Jim Devlin on Testament for DC, and assisting Ian Richardson on 2000A.D.'s Sinister Dexter. His inks and colors will also be featured in Platinum's graphic novel *Final Orbit*. He's currently writing three creator-owned series.

He lives on the west coast of Scotland.